INSIGHT ⊙ GUIDES

EXPLORE

CANADA

T0154431

PROMOTIONAL FEATURE

PLAN & BOOK
YOUR TAILOR-MADE TRIP

BRAZIL **CHILE** **ECUADOR**

TAILOR-MADE TRIPS & UNIQUE EXPERIENCES CREATED BY LOCAL TRAVEL EXPERTS AT INSIGHTGUIDES.COM/HOLIDAYS

Insight Guides has been inspiring travellers with high-quality travel content for over 45 years. As well as our popular guidebooks, we now offer the opportunity to book tailor-made private trips completely personalised to your needs and interests. By connecting with one of our local experts, you will directly benefit from their expertise and local know-how, helping you create memories that will last a lifetime.

HOW INSIGHTGUIDES.COM/HOLIDAYS WORKS

STEP 1

Pick your dream destination and submit an enquiry, or modify an existing itinerary if you prefer.

STEP 2

Fill in a short form, sharing details of your travel plans and preferences with a local expert.

STEP 3

Your local expert will create your personalised itinerary, which you can amend until you are completely satisfied.

STEP 4

Book securely online. Pack your bags and enjoy your holiday! Your local expert will be available to answer questions during your trip.

PROMOTIONAL FEATURE

BENEFITS OF PLANNING & BOOKING AT INSIGHTGUIDES.COM/HOLIDAYS

PLANNED BY LOCAL EXPERTS

The Insight Guides local experts are hand-picked, based on their experience in the travel industry and their impeccable standards of customer service.

SAVE TIME & MONEY

When a local expert plans your trip, you save time and money when you book, even during high season. You won't be charged for using a credit card either.

TAILOR-MADE TRIPS

Book with Insight Guides, and you will be in complete control of the planning process, from the initial selections to amending your final itinerary.

BOOK & TRAVEL STRESS-FREE

Enjoy stress-free travel when you use the Insight Guides secure online booking platform. All bookings come with a money-back guarantee.

WHAT OTHER TRAVELLERS THINK ABOUT TRIPS BOOKED AT INSIGHTGUIDES.COM/HOLIDAYS

Trip to Portugal

Every step of the planning process and the trip itself was effortless and exceptional. Our special interests, preferences and requests were accommodated resulting in a trip that exceeded our expectations.

Corinne, USA   ★★★★★

Trip to Vietnam

The organization was superb, the drivers professional, and accommodation quite comfortable. I was well taken care of! My thanks to your colleagues who helped make my trip to Vietnam such a great experience.

Heather   ★★★★★

DON'T MISS OUT
BOOK NOW AT
INSIGHTGUIDES.COM/HOLIDAYS

CONTENTS

COVID-19 updates

While travelling in Canada, be sure to heed all local laws, travel advice and hygiene measures. While we've done all we can to make sure this guide is accurate and up to date, be sure to check ahead.

CHILDREN

Vancouver has a vast aquarium and harbour whale-watching tour (Route 10), New Brunswick offers zip-lining thrills over its natural whirlpools (Route 3) and Montreal packs in fun with its Ferris wheel and science centre (Route 4).

RECOMMENDED ROUTES FOR...

FOOD AND WINE

Red, white or ice? Uncork them all in Niagara-on-the-Lake (Route 5). Toronto's St Lawrence Market has the best fresh produce (6), while Vancouver (Route 10) takes the crown for top cocktails and farm-to-table cuisine.

HISTORY HUNTERS

The world of fur traders, whiskey traders and Canadian Mounties is brought to life at Fort Walsh National Historic Park (Route 8), as is the gold rush-era at the site of the stampede, Dawson City (Route 12).

PERFORMING ARTS

Get merry to the tune of folk musicians on Routes 1 and 2. Experience Toronto's theatre scene at the Distillery District (Route 6), and Montreal's entertainment hub, Quartier des Spectacles (Route 4).

ROAD TRIPS

Explore the beautiful and highly accessible east coast roads (Routes 1, 2 and 3), cut through epic Rockies scenery (Route 9) or link up two legendary Yukon cities on the Klondike Highway (Route 13).

SNOW ACTIVITIES

Slide into the Snow Castle at Yellowknife's winter festival (Route 14), try out cross-country skiing in Cypress Hills (Route 8) and camp in the Arctic, on Baffin Island's floe edge (Route 15).

WILDLIFE

Fall means polar bear-spotting season in Churchill (Route 7), while summer draws visitors to trace rare wildlife in Nunavut (Route 15), and migrating whales at PEI (Route 3) and Haida Gwaii (Route 11).

INDIGENOUS CULTURE

The Haida's close-to-nature lifestyle in a splendid setting beckons visitors in Route 11; or get to know the fascinating culture of the Indigenous People of the North in Routes 7 and 15.

INTRODUCTION

An introduction to Explore Canada's geography, customs and culture, plus illuminating background information on cuisine, history and what to do when you're there.

EXPLORE CANADA

Some of the most astonishing scenery on Earth stretches across its second biggest country, embellished by cities that flourish with creativity and culinary clout. It's time to put all modesty aside, because Canada has a great deal to shout about.

Even for most Canadians, the immense size of the country is hard to appreciate. The nation spans over 5,500km (3,400 miles) from the Atlantic Ocean to the Pacific and over 4,600km (2,900 miles) from the northern tip of Ellesmere Island to the United States border.

This sprawling country is not, of course, fully inhabited: 89 percent of the land has no permanent population. Nearly 82 percent of the 35 million Canadians live in large urban centres located within a few hours' drive of the southern border, mostly in Ontario, Québec, or British Columbia.

Covid-19 updates

In early 2020, Covid-19 swept across the globe, being categorized as a pandemic by the World Health Organization in March 2020. While travelling in Canada, be sure to heed all local laws, travel advice and hygiene measures; flouting these means risking your own health but can also put a strain on local communities and their medical infrastructure. While we've done all we can to make sure this guide is accurate and up to date, permanent closures and changed opening hours are likely in the wake of coronavirus, so be sure to check ahead.

GEOGRAPHY AND LAYOUT

Canada is dominated by its three principal cities: Toronto, Montréal, and Vancouver, all near the border with the United States. Montréal, defined by its old-world charm and new-age outlook, with massive modern and postmodern skyscrapers alongside gracious red-brick mansions; Toronto, teeming with street energy, theatres and ethnic restaurants; and Vancouver, on the far west coast, where individuality is a valued trait, and the pioneer spirit of a young culture pervades every aspect of life.

In between, and north of the cities, lies an expanse of cinematic scenery. At last count, there were 46 national parks, home to wild birds and grizzly bears, four national marine conservation areas, and 42 rivers totalling more than 10,000km (6,250 miles) in the Canadian Heritage Rivers System. Over half the countryside is forest, and trees soaring to a height of more than 60 meters (200ft) are not uncommon.

Prince Edward Island

Rural Canada is divided into 10 provinces and three territories. Newfoundland and Labrador is the most easterly province, in the North Atlantic; Prince Edward Island is the smallest; Nova Scotia is a peninsula; New Brunswick is nearly rectangular with two coastlines; Québec's and Ontario's cities and high-octane profiles make them the best known – although Alberta is fast catching up; in the Prairies, Saskatchewan's reputation for innovation is beginning to match the splendour of its landscapes, although Manitoba is somewhat less exuberant. Time is needed for exploring Canada's three territories: the Yukon, the Northwest Territories and Nunavut.

The main cities have excellent public transport and don't require car hire. When travelling from place to place, domestic air services are preferable, both for travelling long distances and for accessing any particularly remote areas. Railways are good for both short and long distances, although trains take five days to travel the 6,360km (3,950 miles) from Halifax in the east to Vancouver in the west.

Buses are inexpensive and especially good for shorter distances or for getting to small towns not serviced by rail or air. The major bus line, Greyhound Canada, offers a number of travel passes and packages.

If general touring is on the agenda, it is usually straightforward to hire a car. There are also numerous car ferries all over Canada which cross lakes and rivers large and small.

Road trips are often the best way to take in Canada, but non-drivers can enjoy the wilderness too – several of the routes in this book, and sections of many, can be done by train, taxi and bus.

HISTORY

The first Indigenous people arrived during the last Ice Age, across the Bering land bridge between what is now Siberia and Alaska. Facing bitter temperatures and hostile winds, it is a wonder that they survived in such an unfriendly climate. These first Canadians developed a remarkable subsistence technology suited to the brutal environment, and traces of their ancient culture linger. They have come to be known as the Inuit.

The Vikings made it to Newfoundland more than 1,000 years ago, but European interest most notably begins in 1497, when John Cabot sailed west and

Indigenous Canada

This guide describes places that include the traditional lands, unceded territories and Treaty territories of Indigenous Peoples, including First Nations, Métis, and Inuit. Travelling offers us the privilege of being a guest among our hosts and building relationships with them. Take the opportunity to learn the history of a place; support Indigenous businesses and artists; and make connections with the people who continue to inhabit these lands.

One of Canada's brown bears takes a rest

sighted Newfoundland and Cape Breton. By the end of the sixteenth century, the British and French pretty much controlled the cod fishery here and Newfoundland became an early focus of Anglo-French rivalries. Meanwhile, in 1535, Frenchman Jacques Cartier encountered the Haudenosaunee (Iroquois) peoples, on the site of Québec City, and later at today's Montréal. Between 1603 and 1635, Samuel de Champlain played a major role in establishing "New France."

Canada wasn't fully unified until 1949 and thus is a country of intertwining histories, rather than a single national thread. Not only does each of its provinces maintain a considerable degree of autonomy, but each grouping of First Nations, Inuit

DON'T MISS OUT ON...

Spotting white giants. Newfoundland's Iceberg Alley is in full "floe" from April to early July, with hundreds of chunks of ice floating past, some around 10,000 years old. Look out for them as you crack into lobster at Doyle Sansome & Sons Ltd, on the coast of New World Island. See page 32.

Dancing at a ceilidh. Translating as "New Scotland" in Latin, Nova Scotia's Highland settlers brought with them traditions that are still alive and well. These group dances happen all over Cape Breton Island during summer and the Celtic Colours festival in mid-October. See page 34.

Playing the tables at Diamond Tooth Gertie's. The world's northernmost casino (and Canada's oldest legal gambling hall) is a Dawson City institution, its gold rush-era theme culminating in cancan and tap-dancing stage shows. See page 90.

Sampling ice wine. Made by leaving the grapes on the vines to freeze in the winter months, Ontario has the perfect conditions to produce it. Get a taste for it at the Peller estate's own igloo-like ice bar, 10Below Icewine Lounge. See page 55.

Hiking at two great lakes in a day. Nothing beats the majesty of turquoise Lake Louise... until you hike up to Peyto Lake Lookout, 45km away, one of the finest vistas in the Rockies with its emerald lake far below. See page 75.

SUP paddleboarding with belugas. You can't get much closer to the wildlife than stand-up-paddleboarding or kayaking with hundreds of beluga whales, which congregate at the mouth of the Churchill River to feed each summer. See page 67.

Going on a bear hunt. The archipelago of Haida Gwaii is home to many endemic species, including the largest subspecies of the American black bear. And at certain times in Churchill, polar bear sightings are practically guaranteed. See pages 82 and 64.

Watching the Northern Lights. Its position under the auroral oval makes the Northwest Territories' capital Yellowknife one of the world's best places to see the swirling greenish-blue lights – and from the comfort of heated outdoor swivel seats. See page 100.

Banff National Park fauna

and Métis peoples can claim a heritage that cannot be easily integrated into the story of white, European Canada. Such a complex mosaic militates against generalization, although Canadians themselves continue to grapple with the nature of their own identity.

CLIMATE

Canada's climate is hugely varied; areas near the coast generally have milder winters and cooler summers than the interior – although winter in the Maritimes Provinces is extremely cold. July and August are reliably warm throughout the country, even in the far north, with September also warm (and busy) in the south (note also that the sun sets much later in the far north in summer).

In Newfoundland, the Maritime Provinces and the North, much of the tourist infrastructure closes from October to May, although winter sports still draw some visitors. The long autumn can be the best time to visit Ontario and Québec, when there are equable temperatures and few crowds. November to March sees sub-zero temperatures almost everywhere except on the West Coast, though winter days in many areas are clear and dry.

The southwestern parts of British Columbia enjoy some of Canada's best weather: the extremes are less marked and the overall temperatures generally milder than elsewhere. Much of the province, though, bears the brunt of Pacific depressions, so this is one of the country's damper regions: visiting between late spring and early autumn offers the best chance of missing the rain.

Summer temperatures average around 24°C (75°F). During July and August, however, the mercury can climb into the 30s (90–100°F) on the prairies and in southern Ontario. In northern Canada, temperatures may stay at 15°C (65°F) during the day, but can drop close to freezing at night.

Winter temperatures average between −5°C and 10°C (10°F and 25°F) from the Maritimes through southern Ontario. It gets colder and windier from northern Québec through the Rockies, with temperatures ranging from −18°C to −5°C (0°F to 10°F). In the Yukon, Northwest Territories and Nunavut, the mercury can drop to as low as −40°C (−40°F). On the balmy southern coast of British Columbia (B.C.), however, warm Pacific currents generally keep the temperature above freezing during the winter at sea level, while snow accumulates at higher levels.

Snowfall varies throughout Canada. Skiers can sometimes take to the slopes and trails by late November, and the snow lasts generally until April or even May in the mountains.

POPULATION

Canada is a spectrum of cultures, a hotchpotch of immigrant groups who supplemented the continent's many Indigenous peoples. The mix that results from its mostly exemplary tolerance is

Justin Trudeau during an election rally

exhilarating, offering such widely differing cultural, artistic and culinary experiences as Vancouver's huge Chinatown, the Inuit heartlands of the far north, the austere religious enclaves of Manitoba, or the Celtic-tinged warmth of the Maritimes.

Throughout history, the varied landscape has had its own particular effect on its inhabitants. The cold, hostile winter environment, bounty of food and availability of land all combined to make Canada both a haven and a hell for its first immigrants. Songs, poems and paintings of early Canada celebrate its compassion and callousness. Yet underlying these themes of survival is the notion of multiculturalism. In 1971, multiculturalism became an official government policy in Canada (and became an act of law in 1988). The policy was designed to reflect one of the original principles of Confederation: that Canada become a system of coordination among different but equal parts: not a "melting pot" but "mosaic."

LOCAL CUSTOMS

Generally, Canadians are polite, tolerant and non-confrontational. It's important to remember your manners here – hold doors open for people following you, don't jump the line and let people get off public transportation before you get on. Perhaps the most obvious variation in Canadian etiquette are the French customs in the province of Quebec. Kissing left and right cheeks is as common as handshaking is elsewhere.

However, from coast to coast, there is no one thing that will mark a person as Canadian except perhaps for the ubiquitous "eh?" everyone seems to use without reservation, as in "It's cold outside, eh?" or "The prime minister's not talking any sense these days, eh?". Ultimately there can be no simple characterization of a people whose country is not so much a single nation as it is a committee on a continental scale.

POLITICS AND ECONOMICS

Leader of the Liberal Party, Justin Trudeau, was sworn in as Canada's Prime Minister in November 2015. Trudeau, then aged 43, acted on several of his campaign promises almost immediately. In a first for Canada, he unveiled a cabinet that is gender-equal – 50 percent women. When asked why, his answer was powerfully simple: "Because it's 2015."

Trudeau moved fast on promised middle class tax cuts, welcomed 25,000 Syrian refugees and appointed an inquiry commission to investigate Missing and Murdered Indigenous Women. His government also legalized recreational cannabis use, pledged to tackle climate change and to usher in a new era of "positive politics."

Despite their identity politics balancing act, one thing is clear: Canadians have an overwhelming sense of pride in their history, their culture and the mesmerizing beauty of their land. Indeed, Canada embraces all this – as well as its own clichés – with an energy that's irresistible.

Samuel De Champlain

Playing at a Calgary park

TOP TIPS FOR VISITING CANADA

Drive safe. In winter, there may be road closures due to snowstorms and avalanches; keep an eye on the rapidly changing weather at www.theweathernetwork.com/ca. Make sure your vehicle is fitted with snow tires and in all seasons, heed Wildlife Warning Signs on roads.

Keep cash. When travelling around rural Canada, it's a good idea to keep cash on you, as you never know where the next ATM will be. Remember to tip 10–15 percent in restaurants, too.

Be bear-aware. Most people blow a whistle while walking in bear country to warn them off. If confronted do not run, make loud noises or sudden movements, all of which are likely to provoke an attack.

Once bitten. Swarms of blackflies (from April to June) and mosquitoes (June until about October) near water can drive you crazy; anything containing DEET should be a reliable repellent. Take three times the recommended daily dosage of vitamin B complex for two weeks before you head into the wilderness to further repel bites.

Get your bearings. All the national and many provincial parks have well-marked and well-maintained trails; however, if you're venturing into the backcountry, try to obtain the appropriate 1:50,000 sheet from the Canadian Topographical Series and equip yourself with GPS. Before setting off on anything more than a short stroll you should be informed of local conditions and properly equipped.

A word on water. Never drink from rivers and streams, however clear and inviting they may look. If you have to drink water that isn't from taps, you should boil it for at least ten minutes, or cleanse it with an iodine-based purifier or a Giardia-rated filter, available from camping or sports shops.

Access all areas. Almost all the national parks have accessible visitor and information centres and many have specially designed, accessible trails. In addition, VIA Rail offers a good range of services for travellers with disabilities – and the larger car-rental companies can provide vehicles with hand controls at no extra charge.

Go fishing. Canada is fishing nirvana. The range of regulations between provinces can be baffling at first, but usually boil down to the need for a nonresident permit for freshwater fishing, and another for saltwater fishing. These are increasingly available online and from most local fishing shops. Short-term (one- or six-day) licences ($15–30) are also available in some provinces ($15–30).

Careful with cannabis. Despite cannabis (marijuana) being legal since 2018, strict regulations remain in place, so check each province's individual rules including where adults can buy it (authorized retailers only), where adults can use it and how much adults can possess (usually a maximum of 30g). Any breach of these rules could lead to arrest and up to fourteen years in jail.

Vancouver Richmond Night Market

FOOD AND DRINK

Seafood suppers in family-run cafes, a burgeoning farm-to-table movement, the cities' plethora of international food and an ever-growing range of local beer and wine – eating and drinking out in Canada has never been so exciting.

The sheer number of restaurants, bars, cafés and fast-food joints in Canada is staggering, with shopping malls, main streets and highways lined with pan-American food chains. Hamburgers and French fries are standard fare on any Canadian thoroughfare, just as in America.

However, it's easy to leave the chain restaurants behind for more interesting options. Today Canada is home to some of the finest chefs in the world, many of whom create "market-inspired" cuisine, relying on the excellence and abundance of local ingredients to craft inspired dishes with blueberries, fiddlehead greens, wild rice, maple syrup, bison and seafood.

Canadian cuisine as a whole is a combination of influences from the native peoples to recent immigrants, using the country's own abundant food resources. If a food or ingredient exists, it's probably available somewhere in Canada, and definitely in the larger cities.

WHERE TO EAT

Farm-to-table restaurants
Canadians are keenly aware of their country's gastronomic resources, and are using more homegrown foods and produce. Indeed, menus have become longer, not because there are more items, but because the descriptions include the provenance of the main ingredients. In Vancouver, the duck will be Polderside, the pork Sloping Hill Berkshire, the oysters Fanny Bay, and the lamb from Salt Spring Island. People here genuinely care about their food and are interested in knowing everything about it.

The environmentally-attuned populace in Vancouver have supported sustainable programs, including Green Table, whose member restaurants commit to reduced waste and more recycling, more eco-friendly practices, and more products that benefit the local economy.

The gourmet influence extends to the Yukon, the Northwest Territories and Nunavut, at least as far as serving tourists is concerned. After decades of canned and packaged foods, people are slowly refocusing on the bounty of the land, including caribou, moose, arctic char and wildfowl.

Modern technology has helped farmers cultivate more exotic foods in Canada profitably, so the bounty that can come out of a local Canadian garden is truly astonishing.

Coffee and croissants

Cafés

Favourites with white-collar workers are café-restaurants featuring wholefoods and vegetarian meals, plus traditional meat dishes and sandwiches too; most have an excellent selection of daily lunch specials for around $10–12. The European-style café, complete with croissants and pain au chocolat, was once to be found only in Montréal, but now such establishments are readily found in all cities and many smaller towns.

Diners

Outside of cities, you're likely to find yourself at family-owned restaurants, cafés or bistros, where prices might be cheaper but the quality of the food is often no less impressive than what you'd find in a metropolis. All over Canada, breakfast and brunch is a serious matter, and with prices averaging between $8 and $15 it's often the best-value and most filling meal of the day. Mountainous meaty sandwiches are common – Quebec puts its own twist on them with its smoked meat sandwiches. A beloved staple of Montreal's snack joints is poutine – fries covered in melted mozzarella cheese or cheese curds and gravy, and its bagels come a close second to New York's.

Pubs

Pubs and bars aren't a bad place to grab a meal either, and they can be great places to get a feel for the neighbourhood's local character. If what they offer is not overly inventive (chicken wings, variations of burger, fish and chips), you can at least bet it will be filling.

Regional specialities

At local, family-run restaurants, you are likely to find regional specialties. These dishes are ones the whole country enjoys

Vancouver street food

The star in Canada's culinary crown is Vancouver: its food scene is hard to beat, and in recent years it's eked out a reputation for having one of the best restaurant scenes in the world.

It's not just the city's restaurants that have caught international attention. The food cart craze is like nowhere else: there are more than 100 trucks around the city and regular Food Truck events (see www.yvrfoodfest.com) selling healthy, culturally diverse foods ranging from Korean-Mexican fusion to El Salvadorian *pupusas*. Check the StreetFoodApp (www.streetfoodapp.com/Vancouver) for opening times and locations.

A summer highlights for foodies is Vancouver's Richmond Night Market, which attracts 20,000 visitors a night on busy weekends and is the only market of its kind in North America. Join the hordes snacking on fresh-cooked Asian street food as the sun sets over nearby YVR airport. You'll find everything from "potato tornados" (deep-fried potatoes sliced wafer thin and wound around a stick) to *takoyaki* (octopus-stuffed creamy dough balls).

Prince Edward Island giant lobster

and that people often use as a shorthand to define a region and its culture. Regional favourites include digby scallops in Nova Scotia, lobster suppers in Prince Edward Island, and Calgary's beef steaks.

Québec is renowned for its outstanding French-style cuisine, and pork forms a major part of the local diet, both as a spicy pâté known as *creton*, and in *tourtière*, a minced pork pie. There are also all sorts of ways to soak up maple syrup – *trempette* is bread drenched with it and topped with fresh cream.

It's no surprise that in the Maritimes, seafood is excellent everywhere, either on its own or in a fish stew or clam chowder. Nova Scotia is famous for its blueberries, Annapolis Valley apple pie, "fat archies" (a Cape Breton molasses cookie) and rappie pie (an Acadian dish of meat or fish and potatoes).

Newfoundland's staple food has traditionally been cod fish, usually in the form of fish and chips, though with supplies dwindling, this has become more of a luxury. More common are salmon, haddock, halibut and hake, supplemented by more bizarre dishes like "cod tongues" (actually the meat in the cheek), "jiggs dinner" (salted beef and vegetables), and fish and brewis (salt cod with hard bread, softened by pork fat and molasses).

The Arctic regions feature caribou (reindeer) steak. Here and there, there's also the odd Indigenous peoples' restaurant, most conspicuously at the Wanuskewin Heritage Park in Saskatoon, Saskatchewan, where the restaurant serves venison, buffalo and black-husked wild rice.

International flavour

There are more than 80 cultural communities, and some 5,000 restaurants at any given time in a city such as Toronto, where the Italian population rivals a midsize Italian city and the Chinatown is one of the busiest in North America.

Asian food is incredibly popular for lunch in every big city. Between about 11.30am and 2.30pm, many restaurants offer special set menus that are generally excellent value. In Chinese and Vietnamese establishments, for example, you'll frequently find rice and noodle dishes, or buffets for $10–15, and many Japanese restaurants serve sushi very reasonably for under $20.

What you can expect in Canada is a cuisine that's like an orchestra, with native and colonial strands and a plethora of richly varied imports. Churrasco-style (Portuguese) barbecued chicken can coexist with Jamaican ginger beer,

---

Food and drink prices

Throughout this guide, we have used the following price ranges to denote the approximate cost of a two-course meal for one with a glass of house wine:

$$$$ = above $70
$$$ = $50–70
$$ = $30–50
$ = below $30

A Canadian Caesar   *Smoked meat sandwich*

as can Armenian *lahmajoon* (flatbread spread with ground lamb) with Thai salad and real ale from a microbrewery.

DRINKS

Tea and coffee
Ubiquitous coffee and doughnut chain Tim Hortons is a staple all over Canada, but in the cities, look out also for specialist coffee shops, where the range of offerings verges on the bewildering. As a matter of course, coffee comes with cream or half-and-half (half-cream, half-milk) unless you ask for skimmed milk or black. Tea, with either lemon or milk, is also drunk at breakfast, especially in the Maritimes.

Beer
Part of the Canadian stereotype is beer, along with back bacon, hockey, and winter. While the rest may be questionable, the beer part has a ring of truth. Canada has a long brewing tradition, initially dominated by Molson and Labatt's. By and large, the major Canadian beers are designed to quench your thirst rather than satisfy your palate. But since the 1980s, microbreweries have grown up, focussing on offering natural beers of distinction and taste, and brew-pubs across the entire country now produce an array of specialty beers.

The big breweries have formed alliances with (or been bought outright by) international consortiums, so the quest for a truly "Canadian beer" leads the discerning drinker to the craft breweries.

Passionate beer devotees now make the discovery of each town's best beer an exciting adventure as important as any museum, park or historic site.

Wine
Canadian wines are fast developing an excellent reputation, particularly those from Ontario's Niagara-on-the-Lake region and BC's Okanagan Valley. Imported wines from a wide range of countries are also readily available and not too pricey. Ontario and British Columbia wines consistently win major international awards. The quality assurance program VQA (Vintner's Quality Assurance) ensures that labelled wines come from specified lands as well as pass sensory tests to confirm varietal characteristics.

Spirits
Globalization has had its influence on the bar scene in cities across the country, so vodka rules, but more as a statement of identity. Downtown bars in Toronto and Vancouver frequently boast selections of single malt whiskies to rival anything in Edinburgh.

Whether it's a classically Canadian Caesar with its clam and tomato (Clamato) juice, tabasco and Worcestershire, or an espresso Martini, Canadians like to make statements with their choice of drink. Canada, despite high taxes on alcohol, boasts some of the most ardent supporters of the highest quality products.

An Arcade Fire concert

ENTERTAINMENT

Canadians have worked with great determination to create a vibrant artistic, dramatic and literary scene that reflects the talents of its multicultural population. Meanwhile, in the world of music, the country has leaders in all genres.

Although artistically Canada is a young nation, its contribution to the arts world is impressive. It has renowned writers, respected literary events and drama festivals, and boasts much-admired theatre and dance, having spawned exceptional classical performers, along with mainstream and alternative composers and performers. Exports of exceptional homegrown talent are on the rise, while the nation's diverse creativity and penchant for joie de vivre delivers a lot to enjoy on our doorstep.

LIVE MUSIC

In the land of Arcade Fire, Drake and k.d. lang, the music scene in Canada is consistently varied. Outdoor concerts are an important part of the summer, with rock concerts featuring the best of national and international performers. Jazz and blues festivals attract thousands across the country, as far north as Dawson City in the Yukon. Celtic-style music is popular in the Atlantic provinces, with Cape Breton fiddlers Ashley MacIsaac, the late Jerry Holland, and Natalie MacMaster finding fame, along with Newfoundland band, Great Big Sea.

Top places to see upcoming Canadian stars include the Horseshoe Tavern in Toronto, Club Soda in Montréal, and the Commodore Ballroom in Vancouver. Toronto exhibits a flourishing live music scene, having become a centre for new and alternative music in North America. A wide-ranging programme of opera and classical music also spans the country.

THEATRE

More and more Canadian plays are being written and performed, including noteworthy work by Indigenous playwrights Tomson Highway (The Rez Sisters) and Drew Hayden Taylor (Toronto at Dreamer's Rock). In Toronto, the theatre scene is the third-largest in the English-speaking world after London and New York. Its comedy club acts are broadcast worldwide and have nurtured such talents as Dan Aykroyd, Jim Carrey and Martin Short.

The Stratford Shakespeare Festival in Ontario attracts an audience of half a million to its annual six-month season, presenting Shakespeare's plays, a variety of musicals, and contemporary classics in four separate theatres. Other popular summer Shakespeare festivals

K–Days Parade in Edmonton

include those held in St John's, Halifax, Saskatoon, Calgary and Vancouver.

FILM

Toronto has an excellent art-house cinema culture. This befits a city that hosts what is often regarded as the world's best film fest, the renowned Toronto International Film Festival, a star-studded ten-day affair in September. Vancouver International Film Festival is another highly rated film fest, where many of the city's art-house cinemas join forces to host the annual showcase of more than 150 films.

Both cities are also major movie and TV show location sites, doubling for various US destinations, to the extent they've each been dubbed the "Hollywood of the North." Toronto, especially, can be frequently seen on screen as "New York".

NIGHTLIFE

Canadians like to let their hair down, and pubs and bars have sprung up in even the most remote neighbourhoods. Vancouver's clubs are more adventurous than in many other Canadian cities, with a varied and cosmopolitan blend of live music. Summer nightlife often takes to the streets, with outdoor bars and (to a certain extent) beaches becoming venues in their own right. Montréal's cabarets and nightlife keeps going strong into the small hours – even bars are open until 3am. Toronto lights up with thriving nightlife as the sun sets, from dusty dive bars to cocktail lounges and craft beer halls.

LGBTQ NIGHTLIFE

Toronto has not one but two LGBTQ neighbourhoods, Gay Village and Queer West Village, both of which have thriving nightlife scenes. Montreal's Le Village gai features camp cabaret and drag shows. In Vancouver's Davie Street Village, you'll find nightlife as colourful as Canada's only permanent rainbow crosswalk, while Edmonton's Jasper Avenue has a fledgling scene of LGBTQ bars and clubs.

Festivals

Every province seems to have its own festival, or several, ranging from heritage themes to celebrations of the seasons. Provincial tourist offices can provide free festival and events calendars for each region. In winter, popular festivals include Banff/Lake Louise Ice Magic Festival (ski races, skating parties, the incredible International Ice Sculpture Competition on the shores of Lake Louise, and Winterlude Ottawa (activities such as ice sculpting, snowshoe races, ice boating and skating for all on the canal). Summer has the most festivals, including the Calgary Stampede in July, one of the biggest rodeos in the world. There are also Highland games in Fredericton and Moncton in New Brunswick in June, Maxville, Eastern Ontario, and Antigonish, Nova Scotia, both in July.

Canadian rodeo show

OUTDOOR ACTIVITIES

*Canadians work hard – but leisure is a serious business too. From skiing and skidoo–
riding to canoeing and camping, and with four distinct seasons to enjoy, the ways
Canadians embrace their outdoor playground are as varied as the landscape itself.*

It is logical that Canadians associate leisure time with time being in the outdoors. After all, the landscape is magnificent, whether it's the rocky coast of Newfoundland, the boreal forest of the north or the ranges of mountains in both east and west. Canadians embrace hiking and cycling in summer, along with water sports that range from swimming to sailing and fishing.

However, people here equally embrace winter – sub-zero temperatures are no obstacle to fun, it's just that activities and venues change. Meanwhile, on the West Coast, residents are smug about being able to ski and sail on the same day.

HIKING

Canada boasts some of North America's finest hiking opportunities, and whatever your ability or ambition, you'll find a walk to suit almost anywhere in the country. All the national and many provincial parks have well-marked and well-maintained trails, and a visit to any park centre or local tourist office will furnish you with adequate maps of easily-followed local paths. Seasoned backpackers can make their own long-distance walking routes by stringing together several longer trails.

SKIING

Wherever there's good hiking, there's also usually skiing. The popular resorts of the Rockies and BC are the main areas, with the top skiing resorts consisting of Banff, Kicking Horse, Big White and Whistler. But there's also great skiing in Québec, especially Mont Tremblant, and a few good runs at the minor day-resorts that dot the other provinces.

ICE-SKATING

Skating is seen as a national pastime. In Ottawa, the citizens anxiously wait for the Rideau Canal to be frozen solid so they can pull out skates and glide from the Parliament Buildings down to Dows Lake, a 7.8km (4.8-mile) journey that makes the canal the largest skating rink in the world.

BIKING

From extreme mountain-biking in the Rockies to a leisure cycle in Ontario's

Kananaskis river rafting

Hockey fans

winelands (see Route 5), the diversity of the terrain means exploring Canada by bike appeals across the board. Nearly 25 years in the making, a coast-to-coast recreational path known as "The Great Trail" (www.thegreattrail.ca) is now open, linking the Atlantic, Pacific and Arctic corners of the nation over 27,000km of trails. Cycling Canada (www.clingcanada. ca) has lots more information on cycling.

CANOEING AND RAFTING

Once a principal means of transportation in Canada, canoeing today is ubiquitous with floating along forest-backed lakes and romantic archipelagos. Seeing the scenery by boat isn't necessarily a tranquil experience though... The rivers of BC offer more demanding rapid routes, while Nahanni National Park in the Northwest Territories just edges Jasper as the top spot for wild white-water thrills.

FISHING

From the Arctic char of the Northwest Territories to the Pacific salmon of BC, excellent fishing can be found in most of the country's abundant lakes, rivers and coastal waters. Many towns have a fishing shop for equipment, and any spot with fishing possibilities is likely to have companies running boats and charters. Most provinces publish detailed booklets on everything that swims within the area of their jurisdiction.

Spectator sports

Catching a classic Canadian sport played live is one of the quintessential experiences here. With players hurtling around and the puck clocking speeds of over 160kph, **hockey** would be a high-adrenaline sport even without its relaxed attitude to combat on the rink (as an old Canadian adage has it: "I went to see a fight and a hockey game broke out"). Tickets start at around $50 for ordinary games, rise to well over $200 for play-offs and nearly always need to be bought in advance.

Canada has four **lacrosse** teams in the National Lacrosse League, or NLL (www.nll.com) – the Toronto Rock, the Calgary Roughnecks, the Saskatchewan Rush and Vancouver Warriors. This is the indoor version of the official national summer sport (it was played by Indigenous people over 500 years ago) and all four draw good crowds. Tickets aren't hard to get in any of the four cities, with the cheapest ranging from $22–30.

Professional Canadian **rodeo** tournaments are as big as their US counterparts, and just as much fun. If you're looking for an alternative to big-league professional sports, this is a good option. Rodeos generally take place in the western provinces (Alberta, BC and Saskatchewan), and are organized by the Canadian Professional Rodeo Association (www.rodeocanada. com). The season runs March–November. Prices can be as low as $10, rising to well over $100 for the finals.

BEST ROUTES

GROS MORNE NATIONAL PARK TO FOGO ISLAND

Drive up to this sensational national park and take a boat trip on Newfoundland's most jaw-dropping lake, hemmed in by 600-metre walls of rock. On the north coast in early summer, there's a high chance you'll spy giant icebergs in the inlets.

TIME: 2.5 days
DISTANCE: 773km (480 miles)
START: Deer Lake Airport
END: Tilting, Fogo Island
POINTS TO NOTE: Ferries connect Newfoundland with Nova Scotia. Watch out for moose: Newfoundland has thousands of them. They present a real danger to the motorist at dawn and dusk. You need a car to make the most of Newfoundland, though it is possible to travel by bus or taxi. The only long-distance bus on Newfoundland is operated by DRL Coachlines (tel: 709 263 2171, www.drl-lr.com), a once-daily service running between Channel-Port aux Basques to St John's via the Trans-Canada Hwy, stopping at over twenty places. A patchy transport network is provided by a string of minibus/taxi companies. Reserving in advance is crucial in July and August, and also in winter, when many places are closed.

Newfoundland's natural and historic charms are considerable, yet, aston-ishingly, the island rarely seems busy or crowded. Many visitors fly straight to St John's, which provides the best introduc-tion to island life, not least for its muse-ums, restaurants and folk music scene.

Newfoundland's attractions don't end on the Avalon Peninsula though. Tiny Trin-ity, on the Bonavista Peninsula, is per-haps the most beguiling of all the old outports. Twillingate comes a close sec-ond and Fogo Island remains one of the most traditional. Gros Morne National Park, 700km (434 miles) west of St John's, features wondrous mountains and glacier-gouged lakes.

GROS MORNE NATIONAL PARK

Fly into **Deer Lake domestic airport** ❶ and rent a car for immediate access to the Unesco World Heritage-protected **Gros Morne National Park** ❷, 35km north up road NL-430 (9am–5pm; www.wpc.gc.ca/en/pn-np/nl/grosmorne; kids free). A place of mesmerizing scenery, it features plunging fjords, wild beaches and wizened sea stacks with a backdrop of bare-topped mountains.

Western Brook Pond in Gros Morne National Park

The park's forested lower slopes are home to thousands of moose, woodland caribou and snowshoe hare, and minke whales regularly feed in Bonne Bay. Gros Morne also attracts artists and musicians, highlighted at the **Trails, Tales and Tunes festival** (www.trailstalestunes.ca) held in Norris Point each May.

Most visitors come here during the short summer season (June–Sept), and other times you'll find many services shut – the exception is the peak winter season (Feb–April), when the park experiences another mini-boom in snowmobiling and cross-country skiing.

ROCKY HARBOUR

It's just under an hour's drive on The Viking Trail (road NL-430), heading north and hugging the beautiful East Arm of Bonne Bay, to Rocky Harbour. Gros Morne's largest village, it curves around a sweeping bay, framed by mountains.

Pull up at the main **visitor information centre** (daily: late June to early Sept 8am–8pm; mid-May to late June and early Sept to late Oct 9am–5pm). There are displays on the natural and human history of the park, as well as free maps, brochures on the park's key hiking trails and details of local boat excursions.

Attractions

Around 5km (3 miles) north is the **Gros Morne Wildlife Museum** ❸ (76 Main St North; July and Aug daily 9am–9pm, also open May, June, Sept and Oct at reduced hours; www.grosmornewildlife.com), an artfully presented gallery of all the crowd-pleasers in natural scenes: caribou, moose, fox, sea birds, beaver, black bear and even a giant polar bear (the latter was acquired in Nunavut). All the animals were acquired humanely from the Parks Service.

Hiking

Multiple trails line this route (all are listed at www.alltrails.com); for a moderate challenge – with the end marked by waterfalls tumbling over a limestone staircase – take the **Baker's Brook Fall Trail** ❹ from Berry Hill Campground. It's 10km (6 miles) in total – 5km there and 5km back, and is doable in 2–3 hours. It's just a 10 minute drive from the lighthouse, taking a right back down the Viking Trail and then the first turning on your left.

WESTERN BROOK POND

The remote **Western Brook Pond** ❺, reached by just one access point, 25km (15.5 miles) north of Rocky Harbour beside Rte-430, is one of eastern Canada's most enchanting landscapes: 16km (10 miles) of deep, dark-blue water framed by mighty mountains and huge waterfalls.

From the car park it's a 40-minute (3km/2 mile) walk on a well-maintained trail through forest and over bog to the edge of the lake. When you get to the end, don't skimp on the two-hour boat trip (res-

Male moose in a Gros Morne meadow

ervations required; July and Aug seven times daily; June and Sept daily 12.30pm) operated by Bontours, who also organise serious hikes here. The boat inches its way between the cliffs right to the extreme eastern end of the lake, past several huge rockslides and former sea caves now marooned high above the water.

NORRIS POINT

Orientating yourself back at Rocky Harbour, it's 6km south to **Norris Point** ❻ on the north shore of **Bonne Bay**, at the point where this deep and mountainous fjord divides into its two inlets, East Arm and South Arm. The village was established in 1833. Stop at the **Jenniex House and Lookout** (104 Main St; late June to mid-Sept daily 9am–7pm; free), a 1926 saltbox home high above the bay. It was moved to this spot in 1995, one of the most jaw-dropping locations in the park. Inside you'll find a craft shop, a small museum of local historic bits and pieces upstairs and a traditional "mug up" – tea and muffins with molasses.

Have dinner in **Neddies Harbour**, where it's all about the local flavours at the popular **Black Spruce**, see ❶, while **Cat Stop**, see ❷, is the place to go for live music and drinks.

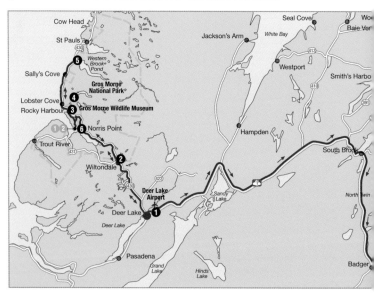

Baker's Brook Falls   *Twillingate*

TRANS-CANADA HIGHWAY

The next morning's drive forms the bulk of this route's distance: a journey of just over 3 hours on the Trans-Canada Highway, back towards the Deer Lake airport and continuing east.

Grand Falls-Windsor

Turn right at Exit 19 and follow the signs for Union Street, then cross the river on Taylor Road for the **Salmonid Interpretation Centre ❼** (100 Taylor Rd; mid-June to mid-Sept daily 8am–8pm; www.erma. ca). On the south bank of the Exploits River 2km (1.2 miles) from the Grand Falls-Windsor centre, this is the best place to see the river's rapids.

The main attraction though, is the 150m (492 feet) fishway, or fish ladder, where thousands of Atlantic salmon leap and fight upstream to spawning grounds at Red Indian Lake. Exhibits in the interpretation centre highlight the history, biology and habitat of salmon, while the observation level provides an underwater view of the migrating fish. Back on Union St, take the next left up the High St for a meal at **Juniper Kitchen & Bistro**, see ❸, or wait until you go through New World Island to dine at **Doyle Sansome & Sons Lobster Pool**, see ❹.

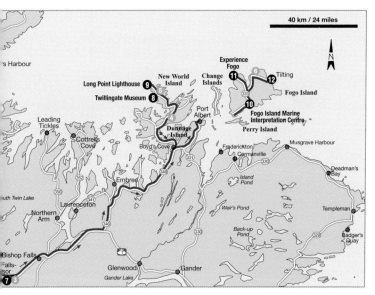

Fogo Island

TWILLINGATE

On to the old fishing port of **Twillingate**, 150km (93 miles) northeast from Grand Falls-Windsor. One of Newfoundland's most popular towns to visit, the romance of the pastel-coloured houses on rocky outcrops is enhanced even more by the causeway that connects it to mainland. Several boat operators compete for tours of frolicking whales in summer and parades of towering icebergs in the spring. If you visit in September, you'll be able to go berry-picking; thousands of bakeapples (cloudberries), partridgeberries (lingonberries) and blueberries smother the slopes around the town. Sample the local fruit wines at **Auk Island Winery**, see ⑤.

Get a sense of the place at the **Twillingate Museum** ⑧ (1 St Peter's Church Rd, off Main St; mid-May to early Oct daily 9am–5pm; donation; www.tmacs.ca), housed in the old rectory.

ICEBERG TOURS

If you are here between late May and early July, the myriad inlets near Twillingate can be studded with vast, shimmering lumps of icebergs as they float down from the Arctic, though in these days of climate change it can be hard to predict their appearance. Check out www.icebergfinder.com for a heads-up on the latest berg activity. Several local companies offer iceberg-watching boat tours, including **Iceberg Quest** (Pier 52, Main St; www.icebergquest.com).

Long Point Lighthouse
Landlubbers still stand a good chance of spotting an iceberg from the bright red and white **Long Point Lighthouse** ⑨ (262 Main St, Crow Head; tel: 709 884 5651) which occupies a commanding position on a high rocky cliff at the tip of Twillingate North Island. Viewpoints and trails lace the headland, and you can climb up the narrow passage to the top of the lighthouse.

FOGO ISLAND

Weathered fish huts, traditional outports and a community of artists occupy **Fogo Island**, one of the most beautifully preserved islands in the province. It is connected to the mainland by a ferry service (4–5 daily 8.30am–8pm; 45 min direct or 1hr 15min via Change Islands), from the tiny port of **Farewell**, an hour's drive on the NL-340 road, with two lefts to pick up the 331 and then the 335. Try to get to the port an hour before departure to ensure you get on – if it's full you'll have to wait for the next one (no reservations).

Just a short ride from the ferry in the village of **Seldom**, visit the **Fogo Island Marine Interpretation Centre** ⑩ (79 Harbour Drive, off Hwy-333; June–Sept daily 10am–4pm), with the 1913 White Retail Store next door now a fishing museum.

Fogo is an extremely picturesque place, surrounded by rocky hills and containing several historic churches, notably **St Andrews,** dating from 1841. You'll pass the church on your right as you drive north to the **Experience Fogo** ⑪ (5–7

Iceberg tour

North Shore Rd; June–Sept 10am–6pm; free) site, an atmospheric collection of wooden buildings preserved to give a sense of the town's fishing heritage.

Tilting

Visit just before the sun goes down, and you may not want to leave the bewitching village of **Tilting** ⑫. Gorgeous clapboard cottages, saltboxes, creaky wharves and boathouses cling to the rocks around the placid harbour. The best way to soak it up is to just wander the streets; though if the sun is out, you should also make a trip to Sandy Cove Beach, one of Canada's best stretches of sand.

If you're looking for a place to eat on Fogo, try **Scoff**, see ⑥.

Food and drink

① THE BLACK SPRUCE

7 Beach Rd, Neddies Harbour; www.theblackspruce.ca; Tues–Sun 5–9pm; $$$$

The Black Spruce serves superb gourmet dinners, featuring such delights as sweet potato soup, Newfoundland mussels, rack of lamb and local desserts like steamed carrot pudding.

② CAT STOP

2–4 Stones Lane, Norris Point Waterfront; tel: 709 458 3343; June–Sept daily 8.30am–8pm (Fri–Sun until 1am)

This pub and café has a sun-drenched upper deck, perfect for early drinks and light snacks after a boat trip. It also hosts live folk music in the evenings.

③ JUNIPER KITCHEN & BISTRO

48 High St; tel: 709 393 3663; daily 10am–2pm and 5–10pm; $$

The best restaurant in town – you won't find better quality: the seafood chowder and Atlantic salmon fillet are excellent, but it's always worth asking about the nightly specials.

④ DOYLE SANSOME & SONS LOBSTER

25 Sansome's Place Hillgrade, Twillingate; www.sansomeslobsterpool.com; early May to early Oct, noon–9pm; $$

Crack into a lobster fresh from the bays and inlets of Newfoundland's northeast coast. Located at the water's edge, look out for whale blow holes and icebergs as you feast. Cash only.

⑤ AUK ISLAND WINERY

29 Durrell St; www.aukislandwinery.com; daily 9.30am–6.30pm Oct–April Mon–Fri 10am–4pm; $$

Visit this local winery for an introduction to the island's growing number of eminently drinkable fruit wines. Winery tours and tastings are also available.

⑥ SCOFF

159 Main Rd, Joe Batt's Arm; late May to mid-Oct Wed–Sat 5.30–9.30pm (longer hours July and Aug); tel: 709 658 3663, www.facebook.com/scoffrestaurant; $$

Best eating on the island, with finely crafted dishes – always ask about local specials such as toutons and beans or jiggs dinner.

CAPE BRETON ISLAND

*Make tracks by causeway and highway to Cape Breton Island –
a major focus for Gaelic and Acadian culture, where the intersecting
Ceilidh Trail and Cabot Trail deliver Atlantic Canada's most scenic
road–trip, around misty forests and a rugged coast.*

DISTANCE: 596km (370 miles)
TIME: 3 days
START: Port Hastings
END: Louisbourg
POINTS TO NOTE: Local tourist offices
will gladly advise you on upcoming
gigs, whether it be a ceilidh, concert
or square dance, and listings are
given in the weekly *Inverness Oran*
(www.invernessoran.ca), a local
newspaper available at tourist offices
and convenience stores. Cape Breton's
weather is notoriously unpredictable,
even in summer, so if possible it's
best to build a bit of flexibility into
your itinerary. This route is seasonal;
attractions and many restaurants are
only open between May and October. To
reach the island, all traffic has to cross
the 1.4km (0.8 mile) Strait of Canso
causeway (free). Public transport to
Cape Breton Island is plentiful, however,
without your own transport, getting
around the island can be a struggle
(Transit Cape Breton offers a limited bus
service; www.cbrm.ns.ca/transit).

From the lakes, hills and valleys of the
southwest to the ripe, forested mountains
of the north, the island offers the most
exquisite of landscapes, reaching its mel-
odramatic conclusion along the fretted,
rocky coast of the Cape Breton Highlands
National Park. Encircling the park and
some of the adjacent shore is the Cabot
Trail, reckoned to be one of the most
awe-inspiring drives on the continent.

The Scottish Highlanders who settled
on Cape Breton in the late 18th and early
19th centuries (many as a result of the
Highland Clearances, where they were
forcibly evicted by landowners) brought
with them strong cultural traditions,
today best recalled by the island's many
musicians.

THE CEILIDH TRAIL

The Ceilidh Trail (ceilidh translating as
"party") starts immediately on Route 19
from **Port Hastings** ❶ as you enter the
island, which hugs the west coast of Cape
Breton Island along the Gulf of St. Lawrence in Inverness County. It takes about
two hours to drive, stretching for 112km

Cape Breton coastline

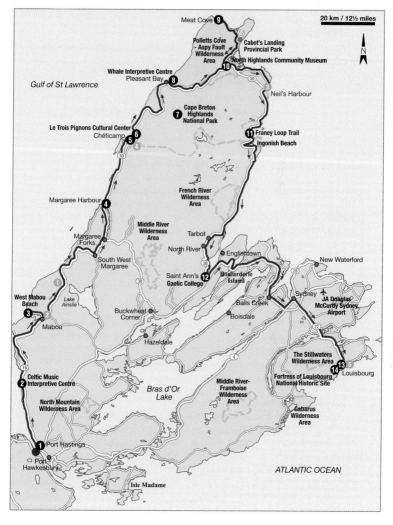

Pastoral Cape Breton

(69.5 miles) until it intersects the Cabot Trail at Margaree.

If your trip is starting on a Sunday, get straight into the swing of things by booking onto the Sunday Ceilidh at the **Celtic Music Interpretive Centre ❷** (2–5pm; www.celticmusiccentre.com/events/index.htm) in **Judique**. At around 28km (17 miles) drive into your journey, you'll see a sign for the Centre. These high-energy group dances, always to live Celtic music, happen at venues all over the island during summer and October's Celtic Colours festival.

Mabou

Otherwise, the first stop is **Mabou**, a 45-minute drive (58km/36 miles). Turn left down Little Mabou Road and pull up in the free parking lot for a walk on **West Mabou Beach ❸**. This quiet, dune-backed sandy beach slopes gently into the sea (which is noticeably warmer than other Cape Breton beaches) – so slip off your shoes for a paddle.

Mabou may be a small rural village, but it's worth lingering here for the evening entertainment in season. If time permits, you could take an Uber to and from the **Glenora Inn & Distillery**, 10 minutes away by car, to discover Cape Breton whisky, see ❶. The Saturday-night Family Square Dance at **West Mabou Hall** (9pm–midnight) is especially well regarded. But a must is an evening at the legendary **Red Shoe Pub**, see ❷, where feet stomp to Celtic bands seven nights a week.

THE CABOT TRAIL

Continue driving north for 60km/37 miles (around 50min) and at **Margaree Habour ❹**, the Ceilidh Trail (road 19) turns into the Cabot Trail (road 30) – offering captivating views of land and sea as it slices across the wide grassy littoral.

The scattered dwellings hereabouts form **La Région Acadienne**, an Acadian enclave established in 1785 by French settlers deported from elsewhere in the Maritimes. Despite being surrounded by English-speaking settlements, the region was connected to the rest of Nova Scotia by road only in 1947, partly explaining the survival of Acadian culture.

Chéticamp

After 30km or so, the road slips into the district's main village, **Chéticamp ❺**. Park up and walk to 15114 Main St. Dominating the heart of Chéticamp is the soaring silver steeple of l'Église Saint-Pierre, completed in 1893 with stones lugged across the ice from Chéticamp Island, just offshore.

Museum

Drive on to **Les Trois Pignons Cultural Center ❻** (15584 Main Street, open daily: mid-May to June and Sept to mid-Oct 8.30am–5pm; July and Aug 8.30am–6.30pm; www.lestroispignons.com) at the north end of the village, beside a golf club. The cultural centre includes the Museum of the Hooked Rug and Home Life, which proudly displays

Chéticamp   *Beach boardwalk*

Acadian artefacts (with detailed explanations) collected by local eccentric Marguerite Gallant, as well as the hooked mats of local artist Elizabeth LeFort.

Stop at **Le Gabriel**, see ❹, (15424 Main Street) for lunch, marked by a replica lighthouse. Afternoons frequently see live music at nearby pub **The Doryman,** including Saturday fiddle performances**.**

CAPE BRETON HIGHLANDS NATIONAL PARK

Drive 9km north of Chéticamp and you'll enter **Cape Breton Highlands National Park** ❼ (www.pc.gc.ca/en/pn-np/ns/cbreton). The extensive park offers some of the most mesmerizing scenery anywhere in the Maritimes – a mix of deep wooded valleys, rocky coastal headlands, soft green hills and boggy upland. Although visitors get a taster of the park travelling by car – 120km (74.5 miles) of Cabot Trail trimming its northern edge – the essence of the place is best revealed on foot, so carve out time to pull up and look around.

The beautiful spot of **Pleasant Bay** is a popular place to set off on seal and whale-watching tours, with its marine theme culminating at the small and friendly **Whale Interpretive Centre** ❽ (104 Harbour Rd; https://whale-interpretive-centre.business.site).

Meat Cove

To get off the beaten track and enjoy the splendour of the National Park in all its drama, press up to the tip of the island, **Meat Cove** ❾. Clouds graze the forested mountains and cliffs jut out into the ocean like something from A Land Before Time, at the viewpoint at the end of a bumpy 8km/5-mile-long gravel road from the hamlet of **Capstick**.

A sociable stay is **Meat Cove Campground** (2479 Meat Cove Rd). This idyllic campground is full of the roar of the ocean, offers kayaks and its own Chowder Hut Restaurant. Stop en route to grab a bottle of wine and any other provisions at the **Cabot Trail Food Market** (30001 Cabot Trail Road).

Down the east coast

Retrace your route back down to Cape North – but pull up for a moment to stand at the windswept **Cabot Landing Provincial Park**, the spot where John Cabot may have "discovered" North America in 1497.

Dip into the **North Highlands Community Museum** ❿ (29263 Cabot Trail; mid-June to Aug daily 9am–5pm, Sept to late Oct Mon–Sat 10am–4pm; www.northhighlandsmuseum.ca). The museum is an enthusiastic attempt to document the history of the area, with displays on local industries, lighthouses, early settlers, and even a few bits and pieces recovered from the *Titanic*.

From Cape North village, heading east, the Cabot Trail skirts the edge of the national park for 30km. When you reach Neil's Harbour village, a sleepy fishing community where squat white houses

Fortress of Louisbourg

line the shore, make a stop for ice cream. Even on the most overcast days, the flavours at **Neil's Harbour Lighthouse** are tempting, see, ❸.

INGONISH

About 20 minutes on the road from Neil's is the pretty harbour at Ingonish, although don't get out of the car until you reach **Ingonish Beach**, 10km/6 miles further south. It is one of the most enticing in the national park, a thin strip of silky sand facing South Bay.

Around these parts is a highly rewarding trail to tackle: the 7.4km/4.5 mile **Franey Loop Trail** ⓫ (around 3 hours), a steep walk up through the mountains and lakes north of Ingonish Beach. Turn off the Cabot Trail just north of the Clyburn River and follow the fire access road to the parking lot, where the trail is signposted. It may be a challenging hike but it delivers a 360-degree view of the Clyburn Brook canyon and the Atlantic coast.

Most of the wildlife inhabits the inner reaches of the park: garter snakes, redbacked salamanders, snowshoe hares and moose are common, black bear and lynx are rarer, but you might be lucky enough to see a bald eagle overhead.

Gaelic College

Snaking down the east coast south of the Cape Breton Highlands National Park, the Cabot Trail threads its way down the 80km/50-mile-long Gaelic Coast, passing through South Gut St Anne's, the location of **Gaelic College** ⓬ (51779 Cabot Trail Road (Hwy-105), Mon–Fri 9am–5pm; www.gaeliccollege.edu).

The main focus of a visit to the Gaelic College (*Colaisde na Gàidhlig*) is the **Great Hall of the Clans,** which provides potted clan descriptions, exhibits tracing Scotland's military history, and pioneer artefacts from the nineteenth century. Also inside are eight interactive displays highlighting Gaelic language, dancing, piping, music, song, storytelling and textiles. Demonstrations include milling frolics, kilt-making and dancing.

Fortress of Louisbourg National Historic Site

Stringing along the seashore 34km (21 miles) southeast of Sydney, the modern village of **Louisbourg** ⓭ comes alive in the summer months, when tourism supplements modest incomes from lobster and crab fishing. The crowds come for the 18th-century living museum, the **Fortress of Louisbourg National Historic Site** ⓮ (259 Park Service Road; Late Maymid-Oct daily 9.30am–5pm; mid-Octlate May Mon–Fri 9.30am–4pm; www.fortressoflouisbourg.ca), which conjures a strong sense of history.

The site begins 2km (1.2 miles) beyond the village of Louisbourg at the visitor centre, where there's a good account of the fort's history. The French began construction in 1719, a staggeringly ostentatious stronghold to guard the Atlantic approaches to New France. Louisbourg was only attacked twice, but

Cabot Trail scenic highway

it was captured on both occasions; it was levelled in 1760. Rebuilt in the 1960s, today it offers an extraordinary window into 18th-century colonial life, its streets and buildings populated by a small army of costumed role-players. From the visitor centre, a free shuttle bus (June–early Sept only) runs to the fort and settlement, whose stone walls rise from the sea to enclose more than four dozen restored buildings as they were in the 1740s. There are powder magazines, forges, guardhouses, warehouses and the chilly abodes of the soldiers, all enhanced by the dazzling coastal setting.

Allow at least three hours to look round the fortress and sample the authentic refreshments available at the taverns and bakeries. For dinner, try the popular waterfront restaurant **Lobster Kettle** (41 Commercial Street), see ⑤.

You can either linger in Louisbourg or drive the two hours back to **Port Hastings** to close the loop. The Atlantic provinces are connected by car-ferry, so you can also easily combine routes.

Food and drink

① GLENORA INN & DISTILLERY

3727 Highway 19, Mabou; www.glenora distillery.com; $$$
The Americas-meets-the-Highlands at Glenora, famous for producing the first single malt whisky produced in North America: "Glen Breton Rare 8 Year Old". Sip your way around their current stock while you tour the barrels and copper pot stills.

② RED SHOE PUB

11573 Route 19 Mabou; www.redshoepub. com; end of May to mid-Oct; Mon–Wed 11.30am–11pm; Thurs 11.30am–1am; Fri–Sat 11.30am–1am; Sun noon–11pm; $$
Come for the Nova Scotia home cooking (such as steaming bowls of seafood chowder) and stay for the Celtic music. Try the Red Shoe Ale, brewed for them by the Propeller Brewing Company of Halifax.

③ NEIL'S LIGHTHOUSE ICE CREAM

90 Lighthouse Road, New Haven; $
The stuff that Cape Breton romance is made from. Devour a bowl of salted caramel ice cream in a red-and-white lighthouse built in 1899, with a pretty harbour view. Cash only.

④ LE GABRIEL

Main Street Chéticamp; www.legabriel.com; daily 11am–10pm; $$
Sumptuous lobsters, crab legs, shrimp, scallops and a chowder thick with cream, bacon and shellfish: this Acadian restaurant is the best place in the region for seafood.

⑤ LOBSTER KETTLE

41 Commercial Street, Louisbourg; www.lobsterkettle.com; mid-June to early Oct; daily noon–8pm; $$$
Louisbourg's only waterfront restaurant is a solid bet for the local specialities of lobster dinners, snow crab and seafood chowder.

NEW BRUNSWICK TO PRINCE EDWARD ISLAND

A dual-province road-trip that will appeal to all ages: this route begins with activities in New Brunswick and ends in Anne of Green Gables territory on Prince Edward Island – with an abundance of rural Maritime beauty in between.

TIME: 2.5 days

DISTANCE: 515km (320 miles)

START: St Andrews, New Brunswick

END: Cavendish, Prince Edward Island

POINTS TO NOTE: The Fundy coast is a popular holiday spot in the summer, so it's a good idea to book accommodation in advance – most things are closed between November and June. This route is designed for drivers, but the Maritime Bus (tel: 506 672 2055, www.maritimebus. com), runs long-distance services throughout the region from the Saint John terminal at 125 Station Street. There is no public transport to the Fundy National Park. New Brunswick's border with Nova Scotia is not too far from the Confederation Bridge (fee on return journey from PEI), so the three provinces can be easily combined.

The New Brunswick side of the Bay of Fundy is a coastal drive that delivers rich rewards, its revitalized port towns petering out into an untouched region of rugged headlands, crumbling cliffs and dense forests trailing into the sea. The main sights are easily accessed via routes 114 and 111: collectively dubbed the Fundy Coastal Drive.

Meanwhile, Prince Edward Island (PEI) was linked to the mainland by the whopping Confederation Bridge in 1997 and possesses one of the region's most enticing culinary scenes. Leafy, laidback Charlottetown is well worth at least a couple of days, especially as it's just a short hop from the magnificent sandy beaches of the Prince Edward Island National Park.

There is a lot of driving on this route but a lot to see as well, so time in the car is always broken up into small chunks.

ST ANDREWS

Start this route in **St Andrews ❶**, a National Historic Site-protected town at the western edge of the Fundy coast. Founded by Loyalists fleeing an independent America in 1783, St Andrews was transformed into an affluent resort town in the late 19th-century, with

Alma, New Brunswick

manicured gardens and neat rows of pastel-coloured clapboard houses reminiscent of New England.

It's also home to one New Brunswick's major family attractions, just north of the town centre, the **Huntsman Fundy Discovery Aquarium** (1 Lower Campus Road; www.huntsmanmarine. ca; mid-May to mid-Oct daily 10am– 5pm), which gives you an insight into the sea creatures and mammals that thrive in the waters right outside.

If you're here in whale-watching season (minke and finback June–Oct, humpback July–Oct), you may wish to swap the aquarium for marine life in the wild (harbour seals and porpoises are also present year-round). The **main pier** is packed with **boat-tour** companies: trips run 3–4 times a day in peak season and usually require a minimum of six people. Fundy Tide Runners (16 King Street/wharf; www.fundytiderunners.com) operates 7.5m Zodiac boat that zips up close to the whales.

New Brunswick's famously extreme tides can be experienced here too, by driving over to **Ministers Island** from the town's Bar Road. Amazingly, the 1km (0.6 mile) road sandbar is under 4m (14ft) of water at other times of day (see tide times at www.ministersisland.net).

For lunch, the **Garden Café** see ❶, at delightful **Kingsbrae Garden**, is a 5-minute drive southeast of the aquarium. Otherwise, begin driving to Saint John, a 1-hour (103km/64 mile) journey on Bayview Drive, Ghost Road and then Route 1 East, before following the signs from Exit 122.

SAINT JOHN

The largest city in New Brunswick, **Saint John ❷** has resplendent Victorian architecture and thriving industry, including Moosehead Breweries – the last major brewery in Canada owned by Canadians.

The city gained international fame for its impressive **Reversing Falls Rapids** (200 Bridge Road; www.skywalksaintjohn. com; late May–Oct daily 9am–sunset; Nov–late May Tue–Sun 11am– sunset) – essentially a tidal tug-of-war created by a sharp bend in the St

John River, about 3km (1.8 miles) west of the centre.

On the other side of the bridge you'll find the Reversing Falls Rapids Tourist Centre and Skywalk, which includes a stainless steel and glass platform that juts out from the cliff over the river. You can also zipline along the riverbank and over the local seals, with **Saint John Adventures** at 50 Fallsview Avenue (June to late Oct; www.saintjohnadventures.ca).

FUNDY NATIONAL PARK

Bisected by route-114, **Fundy National Park ❸** encompasses a short stretch of the Bay of Fundy's pristine shoreline, all jagged cliffs and tidal mudflats, and the forested hills, lakes and river valleys of the central plateau behind. This varied scenery is crossed by more than 100km

---

The Fundy Footpath

Experienced hikers can tackle the 50km (31 miles) between Fundy National Park and the Fundy Trail Parkway via the spectacular coastal Fundy Footpath (www.fundyhikingtrails.com), accessible from the end of Goose River Path (7.9km/4.9 miles; 2hr 30min) from Point Wolfe in Fundy National Park. The challenging trail ends near the Big Salmon River Interpretive Centre on the Parkway. Most people take four days and camp along the way; all hikers are required to register by calling 866 386 3987.

(62 miles) of hiking trails, mostly short and easy walks taking no more than three hours to complete.

The pick of the trails are along the Fundy shore. From the car park to the south of Point Wolfe Campground you can access the awe-inspiring **Point Wolfe Beach Trail ❹**, a moderately steep, 600-metre (1,986ft) hike down from the spruce woodlands above the bay to the grey-sand beach below (15min).

From the same starting point, the **Coppermine Trail** (1hr 30min–2hr) meanders through the forests with views out along the seashore over a 4.4km (2.7 miles) loop. Birdlife is more common in the park than larger wildlife, though you may see the odd moose, and precocious raccoons in the summer.

Alma

Just outside the perimeter of the park, the sleepy little village of **Alma ❺** is worth stopping at for its wealth of delicious seafood alone (try the **Alma Lobster Shop** at 36 Shore Lane, see ❷).

Hopewell Cape

From **Fundy Highlands Inn** it's 47km (29 miles; around 38min) south along the west bank of the Petitcodiac River on Route-114 to the captivating shoreline of **Hopewell Cape ❻**, contained within the privately managed Hopewell Rocks park (131 Discovery Road; www.thehopewellrocks.ca).

The interpretive centre at the park's upper section explains the cape's geology

Hopewell rocks

and the marine complexities of the Bay of Fundy, but you'll soon be wandering down the footpath to the lower section – past several vantage points – to the gnarled red-sandstone pinnacles known as the Flowerpot Rocks rising up to 15 metres (49 feet) above the beach (golf carts shuttle back and forth for $2 one way).

The rocks were pushed away from the cliff face by glacial pressure during the Ice Age, and the Bay of Fundy tides have defined their present, eccentric shape. At high tide they resemble stark little islands covered in fir trees, but at low tide they look like enormous termite hills. Steps lead down to the beach and you can safely walk round the rocks two to three hours either side of low tide, or paddle round them at high tide by taking a guided tour by kayak (www.baymountadventures.com; June–Aug; 1–2hr tours from $69). Your ticket is valid for two days to ensure you see both tides.

Confederation Bridge

After Hope Cape, the coastline curves north with an inlet, delivering you to Moncton where you take route 15, and then 16, to cross the **Confederation Bridge 7**. Stretching 13km (8 miles), this engineering feat is longest bridge in the world over ice-covered waters. It takes around 10 minutes to drive across.

Leaving the rugged New Brunswick eastern coast behind, you're heading into bucolic Prince Edward Island, the home of Confederation and prized for its postcard-worthy pastures, red-sand beaches and lobster suppers.

PRINCE EDWARD ISLAND

The Trans-Canada Highway will lead you to **Charlottetown 8**. Hopewell Cape to Charlottetown is a drive of 2.5 hours, so pocket-sized Charlottetown provides a good spot to stretch your legs. The administrative and business heart of PEI since the 1760s, it is the most urbane spot on the island, the comfortable streets of its centre hemmed in by leafy avenues of clapboard villas and Victorian red-brick buildings.

In small-island terms, it also offers a reasonable nightlife, with a handful of excellent restaurants and a clutch of lively bars, though the

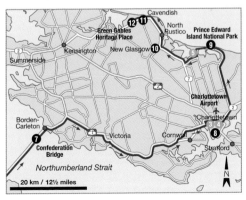

Confederation Bridge

best time to be here is in the summer, when the otherwise sleepy town centre is transformed by festivals, live music and street cafés.

Founders' Hall Market

Founders' Hall Market (6 Prince Street) is a recent addition to the Charlottetown waterfront. Around 20 vendors sell their food and crafts over the hall's 16,000 sq ft (1,486 sq metres), from Rawsome Juice to an oyster bar. It has a mezzanine level upstairs so people can sit and eat-in.

You can hardly come to PEI without tucking into a lobster supper. A good restaurant option is **Water Prince Corner Shop**, see ❸, then walk around the corner for a beer at **Gahan House**, see ❹.

Stock up on snacks for the car at **Anne of Green Gables Chocolates** (100 Queen Street; www.annechocolates.com). The Anne brand was inevitably applied to chocolate in 1999, and this store is chock-full of old-fashioned sweets and handmade chocs (the Cow Chips are highly recommended).

PRINCE EDWARD ISLAND NATIONAL PARK

Either stay the night in Charlottetown, or drive to **Prince Edward Island National Park** ❼. The fastest route to the easterly section of the national park is the half-hour, 23km (14-mile) thump along Route-15, which branches off Route-2 on the north side of town.

Pulling in thousands of visitors every summer, the gorgeous sandy beaches of Prince Edward Island National Park extend along the Gulf of St Lawrence shore for some 40km (25 miles). Facilities (toilets, beach boardwalks, visitor centres, picnic areas and campgrounds) are open from mid-May to October. There's a small charge June–August, but at other times it's free.

Rarely more than a couple of hundred metres wide, the main body of the park incorporates both the beaches and the sliver of low red cliff and marram grass-covered sand dune that runs behind – a barrier which is occasionally interrupted by slender inlets connecting the ocean with a quartet of chubby little bays. The park has 15 short hiking trails, easy strolls that take in different aspects of the coast from its tidal marshes and farmland to its woodlands and dunes.

The next day, drop in for brunch at **Dunes Studio Gallery and Café**, see ❺ – also a shop and art gallery, located just 600 metres (1,968ft) beyond the route-6 and route-15 junction.

New Glasgow

Drive south, away from the National Park and then take the right turning at the white windmill onto Route 6, then the 224 once you've crossed the river. You will find yourself in **New Glasgow** ❿, where a matching pair of black-and-

St Andrews flowers   *Cavendish farmhouse*

white clapboard churches sit on opposite sides of an arm of Rustico Bay.

The reason for stopping here is a culinary one: **Prince Edward Island Preserve Company** (2841 New Glasgow Road; www.preservecompany. com) In the centre of New Glasgow, it's the best place to buy local jams, mustards and maple syrups, and the attached restaurant (daily late May to late Oct) serves first-rate breakfasts, lunches and – in the summer – evening meals.

CAVENDISH

Continue driving from New Glasgow for 10km to Cavendish along Route-13. Next stop is **Cavendish** ⓫, clumped around the junction of Route-6 and Route-13, behind another stretch of fabulous PEI National Park beach. You can walk between the west and east sections of the beach: the west side is better for swimming, while the east is noted chiefly for its crumbling red sandstone headlands.

Yet the reason so many people come to Cavendish is because it lays claim to the key sights associated with the ubiquitous Anne of Green Gables. Even the most jaded travellers spend a couple of hours paying homage to the red-haired, pigtailed orphan girl. The heart-warming books have been a phenomenal worldwide sensation since they were first published in 1908, and the vivid descriptions of rural PEI, captured in the 1985 TV miniseries, has undeniably inspired many a trip here.

Green Gables

From the back of the Lucy Maud Montgomery's Cavendish Home you can walk along the old homestead lane, across Route-13 and along the Haunted Wood Trail into the back of **Green Gables Heritage Place** ⓬, the primary Anne pilgrimage site (8619 Cavendish Road on Route-6; www.pc.gc.ca/en/lhn-nhs/pe/greengables; May–Oct daily 9am–5pm; under 18s free). The main entrance is on Route-6, just 500 metres (0.3 mile) west of Route-13. The two-storey timber house was built in 1831 and was once owned by the Macneill cousins of Montgomery, serving as her inspiration for the fictional Green Gables farm in the novel.

The house has been modified several times since then, and the rooms have been decked out in authentic period furnishings, though few pieces are original to the house – the main aim was to faithfully match descriptions in the book, and Matthew's bedroom, the parlour and Anne's room are littered with items fans will recognize from the story. You can also explore the replica outhouses, and the visitor centre, which contains Lucy's original typewriter and scrapbooks.

On the corner of routes 6 and 13, the old cemetery contains the grave of Montgomery, her husband and her mother.

Anne of Green Gables Museum

Lucy's funeral, held here in 1942, is said to have been the closest thing to a state funeral PEI has ever had.

Families may well also want to check out **Avonlea Village** (8779 Cavendish Road [Route-6] www.avonlea.ca; free), a mock 19th-century village based on Anne of Green Gables' fictitious home, stocked with shops, Cows ice cream and cafés.

Food and drink

🔵 GARDEN CAFÉ

Kingsbrae Garden, 220 King Street, St Andrews; www.kingsbraegarden.com; mid-May to early Oct 11am–4pm (July and Aug to 8pm); $$

Most known for its afternoon tea served from 2.30pm, this café also does great chowder and fresh garden salads. An award-winning fine-dining restaurant, Savour in the Garden, is also on-site.

🔵 ALMA LOBSTER SHOP

36 Shore Lane, off Foster Road, Alma; daily 11am–9pm; $$

Overlooking the water, this shop sells live (by the pound, market price) and cooked lobsters (around $2–3 more); buy one to eat on the picnic tables outside, or get a lobster roll-to-go.

🔵 WATER PRINCE CORNER SHOP

141 Water Street, Charlottetown; www.water princelobster.ca; daily: May, June and Sept to Oct 10am–8pm; July and Aug 10am–10pm; Nov to mid-Dec noon–8pm; $$

It may look like a corner shop, but many locals swear by the seafood here – even if they are usually outnumbered by the tourists. The lobster dinners and chowders are perhaps the best on the island, but the scallop burger is superb too. You can also buy fresh lobsters to go. Moderately priced for the quality of the produce.

🔵 GAHAN HOUSE

126 Sydney Street, Charlottetown; www.charlottetown.gahan.ca; Mon–Wed and Sun 11am–midnight, Thurs–Sat 11am–1am

PEI's microbrewery produces seven crisp handcrafted ales on-site, from the potent Sydney Street Stout to the lighter Harvest Gold Pale Ale. The pub food is equally comforting – try the signature Brown Bag Fish & Chips, ale-battered haddock (yes, served in a brown bag).

🔵 DUNES STUDIO GALLERY AND CAFÉ

3622 Brackley Point Road (Route-15), Brackley Beach; www.dunesgallery.com; daily: June and Sept 11.30am–9pm; July & Aug 11.30am–10pm; Oct 1 to mid-Oct 11.30am–4.30pm; $$$

Part of a cool modern complex featuring a pottery shop and art gallery, Dunes serves meals from an imaginative menu, such as brie and pear pizza and banana bread crumb-crusted halibut.

Place d'Armes

MONTRÉAL

Sometimes described as "half Paris, half Brooklyn", Quebec's biggest city is an exuberant mix of French heritage and cutting-edge creativity. This walking tour centres around Old Montréal, taking in its history, and ends in the dazzling Quartier des Spectacles entertainment district.

DISTANCE: 4.5km (2.8 miles)
TIME: Half day to full day
START: place d'Armes
END: Quartier des Spectacles
POINTS TO NOTE: This route can be as child-friendly (or unfriendly, regarding the late-night venues), as you like. Simply walking around the colourful Quartier des Spectacles is a delight for kids. As a major tourism hub, it's best to book ahead in Montréal for dinner, activities and shows.

Home to over a third of all Québécois, the island metropolis of Montréal celebrates both its European heritage and its reputation as a truly international city. There can be few places in the world where people on the street flit so easily between two or more languages – sometimes within the same sentence – or whose cafés and bars ooze such a cosmopolitan feel.

It's a cliché to describe a destination as a "juxtaposition of old and new", but in Montréal this is spectacularly evident. Canada's second-largest city is

geographically as close to the European coast as to Vancouver, and in look, taste and feel it combines some of the finest aspects of the two continents. Its North American skyline of glass and concrete rises above churches and monuments in a melange of European styles as varied as Montréal's social mix.

VIEUX-MONTRÉAL

This route starts in Vieux-Montréal (Old Montréal), known for its cobblestone streets lined with bars and grand buildings and monuments. North America's greatest concentration of 17th-, 18th- and 19th-century buildings has its fair share of tourists, but it's popular with Montréalers, too – formerly as a symbolic place to air francophone grievances; more recently as a spot to check out the buskers, take in the historic monuments and roam the port's waterfront.

Place d'Armes

The focal point of Vieux-Montréal is **place d'Armes ❶**, a pedestrianized square and statue site of Montréal's founder,

Interior of Basilique Notre-Dame

close to the Metro station of the same name, its centre occupied by a century-old statue of Maisonneuve, whose missionary zeal raised the wrath of the displaced Iroquois. The mutt that you see represents the animal who warned the French of an impending attack in 1644.

Depending on what time of day you start this route, coffee or kombucha might be in order. A good choice is **Paquebot Vieux-Mtl**, see ❶, a three-minute

walk from place d'Armes, on the parallel rue St-Lawrence.

Basilique Notre-Dame

Otherwise, from place d'Armes, cross Notre-Dame Street West (rue Notre-Dame oust) and walk up the steps of the **Basilique Notre Dame** ❷ (www.aurabasiliquemontréal.com; Mon–Fri 8am–4.30pm, Sat 8am–4pm, Sun 12.30–4pm; charge includes 20min guided tour).

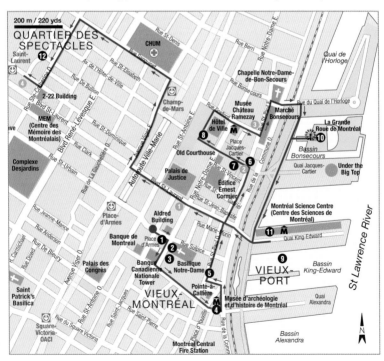

Clock tower   *Place Jacques–Cartier*

This twin-towered, neo-Gothic cathedral of the Catholic faithful has loomed over place d'Armes since 1829. Its architect, the Protestant Irish-American James O'Donnell, was so inspired by his creation that he converted to Catholicism in order to be buried under the church. The western tower, named Temperance, holds the 10-tonne Jean-Baptiste bell, whose booming could once be heard 25km (15.5 miles) away.

Its breathtaking gilt and sky-blue interior, flooded with light from three rose windows unusually set in the ceiling, and flickering with multicoloured votive candles, was designed by Montréal's Victor Bourgeau. The Aura sound and light show offers the chance to see the architectural details artfully lit up (www. basiliquenddm.org; generally 6pm daily, with additional times in summer and on weekends).

Slightly south of place d'Armes, next to the cathedral, the mock-medieval **Séminaire de St-Sulpice ③** (The Old Sulpician Seminary; 110 rue Notre-Dame ouest) sits behind fieldstone walls and wrought-iron gates. It's not open to the public, but stopping by will help you get a sense of the city's history. The low-lying seminary features a portal that's topped by North America's oldest public timepiece, which began chiming in 1701.

Generally considered Montréal's oldest building, it was founded in 1685 by the Paris-based Sulpicians, who instigated the establishment of Montréal by Maisonneuve as a religious mission.

PLACE ROYALE

Take the next left along Saint Francois Xaviour Street. A five-minute walk towards the St Lawrence River will bring you to the **Pointe-à-Callière, Montréal Archaeology and History Complex ④** (350 place Royale; www.pacmuseum. qc; Tue–Fri 10am–5pm, Sat and Sun 11am–5pm; free guided tours generally offered three times daily – check the website for current times).

The sleek, superbly curated museum, which sprawls out underground, focuses on the development of Montréal as a meeting and trading place, as told through the archaeological remains excavated here at the oldest part of the city, as well as high-tech audio-visual presentations. Be sure to leave time for the temporary shows, which cover everything from local gastronomy to the history of the telephone in Québec. The gift shop has a decent stock of distinctive souvenirs.

Along with the neat classical **Old Customs House** on its left as you face the river, the site of the museum forms **place Royale**, where the original colony was established. Duels, whippings and hangings took place amid the peddlers and hawkers who sold wares from the incoming ships in 17th-century New France.

Take the perpendicular street on the far side of **place Royale** and you'll meet the thoroughfare of rue **Saint-Paul West ⑤** (rue St-Paul Ouest), which becomes rue **Saint-Paul Est** as you walk right. Montréal 's oldest street (and

once its main high street) is lined with 19th-century commercial buildings and Victorian lampposts, the buildings little changed from when Charles Dickens stayed here, although they now house restaurants, art galleries and specialist shops selling everything from Inuit crafts to Québécois arts.

Ask a local to recommend a place to find excellent poutine, and this place invariably comes up: **Montréal Poutine**, see ❷, located on your left as you make your way along this street.

Place Jacques-Cartier

After about nine minutes (700m/0.4 mile), turn left along the paved **place Jacques-Cartier** ❻. A popular gathering spot for locals and tourists, the square was originally built as a market in 1804. In the summer are outdoor restaurants and cafés, along with buskers, street artists and caricaturists.

The city-run **tourist office** occupies a stone building at the northwest corner. Take a wander up and down the narrow **rue St-Amable** ❼ to the west, which is dotted with artists selling watercolours and tinted photos of Montréal scenery. A few buildings on the square – Maison Vandelac, Maison del Vecchio and Maison Cartier – show the features typical of Montréal architecture in the 1800s, with pitched roofs designed to shed heavy snowfall and small dormer windows to defend against the cold.

At the top of the square itself looms the controversial **Nelson Monument**.

The city's oldest monument – the column is a third the height of its more famous London counterpart, but pre-dates it by a few years – was funded by anglophone Montréalers delighted with Nelson's 1805 defeat of the French at Trafalgar. Québec separatists adopted it as a rallying point in the 1970s.

Just beyond the statue, you can take a break in the summer by flopping on the grass at **place Vauquelin** ❽. Centred on a pretty fountain and statue of the naval commander Jean Vauquelin, the 1858 place Vauquelin gives views of the Champ de Mars to the north.

OLD PORT OF MONTRÉAL

Facing **City Hall** from the grass, walk forward, moving north a block on rue Saint-Paul Street East and then continuing in your previous direction, to hit the St Lawrence River waterfront. Here is the **Old Port of Montréal (Vieux-Port)** ❾, which extends along the St Lawrence River, from rue McGill to rue Berri.

The Old Port has been turned into a summer playground with landscaped parklands, urban beaches and giftshops facing onto the St Lawrence, but once, it was the principal import and export conduit of the continent. When the main shipyards shifted east in the 1970s they left a lot of vacant space, which in 1992 was fully renovated for public use, with parks, a breezy promenade, biking and jogging paths, exhibitions in the quayside hangars and outdoor restaurants and cafés.

Twilight view of La Grande Roue de Montréal

The Vieux-Port comes into its own in the summer, with a variety of festivals and activities, including an outdoor film festival, obstacle courses and circus acts.

Clock tower

One landmark you can't miss is the white clock tower, rising 51m (167 feet) above sea level. The **Tour de l'Horloge** (Clock Tower) (end May to mid-Sept daily 11am–7pm; free) was built in 1922 to commemorate the men of the Merchant Fleet who died in World War I. The 192 steps leading up to the observatory will reward you with excellent views of the harbour, the St Lawrence Seaway, Vieux-Montréal, the islands and Mont Royal.

In the summer, a sandy beach, **Plage de l'Horloge** (www.oldportofmontréal. com; hours can vary, but generally end May to mid-June Fri–Sun 11am–9pm; mid-June to early Sept Mon and Tues 11am–5pm, Wed–Sun 11am–9pm; charge for special events), opens at the foot of the clock tower, with an outdoor bar.

Family activities

Want to rise above it all? Climb aboard **La Grande Roue de Montréal** ⑩ (www. lagranderouedemontréal.com; daily 10am–11pm), the tallest observation wheel in Canada, which opened in 2017 as part of Montréal's 375th anniversary festivities. Take in sweeping views, from the waterfront to the skyline. Accessed on the same pier as the clock tower, you'll also pass a children's playground as you make your way to the wheel.

If you're travelling with kids, you may want to swap the history museum for the **Montréal Science Centre (Centre des Sciences de Montréal)** ⑪ (quai King-Edward; www.montréalscience centre.com; Mon–Fri 9am–4pm, Sat–Sun 9am–5pm). This family-friendly interactive science and entertainment complex covers everything from the earth and environment to technology, with plenty of hands-on exhibits.

Check in advance, to see if your visit coincides with a performance by Montréal's acrobatic darlings, Cirque du Soleil, who perform in the venue **Under the Big Top** (generally late spring and early summer), located on the pier between the science centre and observation wheel.

When you're in the urban centre of Montréal, it can be easy to forget that it is, in fact, an island. One of the best ways to remind yourself is by taking to the waters. The Vieux-Port is the major departure point for various boat trips. A good-value boat ride is **Le Petit Navire** (quai Jacques-Cartier; www.lepetitnavire. ca; daily departures mid-May to mid-Oct; 45min). These eco-friendly, electric-powered boats whisk tourist off for short tours around the Old Port.

One of Canada's top restaurants is just a four-minute walk back towards the City Hall: **Club Chasse et Pêche**, see ③.

QUARTIER DES SPECTACLES

From King Edward Quay, the pier with the Science Centre, walk directly away

Graffiti on Saint–Laurent Boulevard

from the waterfront on vibrant, ethnically diverse **Saint Laurent Boulevard**, known locally as The Main. Traditionally, boulevard St-Laurent divided the English in the west from the French in the east of the city. It became an "immigration corridor," as Montréal's diverse arrivals settled in the middle. The area around The Main is still a cultural mix where neither of the two official languages dominates (although French is the only official language of Québec.)

After around a 20-minute walk (1.5km/1 mile), The Main will deliver you to Montréal's most lively and exciting place to be once evening sets in,

Quartier des Spectacles ⓬. The city's cultural hub spreads out over square kilometres from the central intersection of Saint-Catherine and St-Laurent.

The theatre, music, dance and art here is astoundingly varied. Dubbed the "Broadway of Montréal", Quartier des Spectacles has over 80 cultural venues and hosts more than 40 festivals. Its signature symbol is a playful red dot, which you'll see throughout – and on the website – a reference to the neighbourhood's former red-light district.

For dinner, a popular choice is the cool Modern European-style restaurant **Cadet**, see ❹.

Food and drink

❶ PAQUEBOT VIEUX-MTL

520 boulevard St Laurent; tel: 514-543-0747; www.paquebot.ca; $
This third wave hip coffee shop knows its beans – but on a summer's day, the lightly carbonised cold lemonade infused with coffee is amazingly refreshing. The setting has a vintage twist, with lofty ceilings and a mezzanine level.

❷ MONTRÉAL POUTINE

181 rue St Paul est; tel: 514-871-9078; 11am–3am; $$
This casual restaurant serves up generous portions of the Montréal classics, smoked meat sandwiches and poutine – or, even better, smoked meat on poutine. Ask to sit

in the decked courtyard when the weather's playing ball.

❸ CLUB CHASSE ET PÊCHE

423 rue St-Claude; tel: 514 861 11122, www.leclubchasseetpeche.com; $$$
The name – "The Hunting and Fishing Club" – is quaintly rural; the food is anything but. A seasonally changing menu may include venison with polenta and aged Cheddar and rabbit ravioli.

❹ CADET

1431 boulevard St-Laurent; www.restaurant cadet.com; 5pm–1am; $$–$$$
Bouillon Bilk's laid-back sister restaurant offers small plates that are full of flavour, such as cod croquettes, blood sausage, and fried burrata, in a chic canteen-style setting.

Niagara-on-the-Lake vineyard

NIAGARA-ON-THE-LAKE WINERIES

Niagara-on-the-Lake is one of Ontario's prettiest towns, but the full extent of this region's charm unfolds when you set off by bike. This is the birthplace of modern Canadian winemaking, and stops at several vineyards can be strung into one loop.

DISTANCE: 24km (15 miles)

TIME: A leisurely full day

START: Queen Street

END: Mississagua Street

POINTS TO NOTE: Call ahead to book tastings at your chosen wineries, allowing plenty of time in the schedule to cycle between each one. This route involves cycling on roads: always wear a helmet, keep to the right-hand shoulder of the road and ride single file. Stick to tastings of the wine (rather than glasses). This itinerary can be combined with the Falls by renting a bike for a second day and cycling south on the Niagara Parkway Recreational Trail (26km/16 miles one-way/around 1 hour 38 mins).

Boasting elegant clapboard houses and verdant, mature gardens, all spread along tree-lined streets, Niagara-on-the-Lake, 26km (16 miles) downstream from the Falls, is used by many as a base for Niagara's major attraction.

However, to remain in its quaint colonial centre is to miss out. It's surrounded by wine country, including some of Canada's leading vineyards, linked up by a combination of bike paths, smooth roads and serene backstreets. With some vineyards dating back to the mid-1970s, the Niagara Peninsula is now the world's largest ice wine region, while also winning awards for its full-bodied reds.

There are 39 wineries within striking distance and you can mix and match as you please – but of course, the closer they are to each other, the more time you can enjoy at each winery. The full list is at https://winecountryontario.ca/winery-listings. Below, we have provided a recommended itinerary of four estates.

QUEEN STREET

It only takes a few minutes to stroll from one end of Niagara-on-the-Lake to the other. The main drag of **Queen Street** is a good place to orientate yourself, with its pretty **clock tower** and the **Niagara Apothecary Museum** ❶ (www.ocp.info; free), which is worth a peep for its beautifully carved walnut and butternut cabinets, crystal gasoliers and porcelain

Cenotaph Memorial in Niagara-on-the-Lake

jars. The area's great tradition of agriculture means farm-to-table is at the heart of the food scene here – best exhibited by the restaurant **Treadwell**, see ❶.

If you have an hour to spare, visit the lovingly maintained **Niagara Historical Museum** ❷ (43 Castlereagh Street; www.niagarahistorical.museum). It holds an enjoyable potpourri of military artefacts as well as an entertaining selection of old photographs and a lively programme of temporary exhibitions on all things local.

Near the other end of Queen Street is the town's finest building, the church of **St Andrews** ❸, at Simcoe and Gage streets, a splendid illustration of the Greek Revival style dating to the 1830s.

BIKE HIRE

There are several bike-hire companies based in the centre of town, including **Zoom Leisure Bikes** ❹ (431 Mississauga Street), close to the start of this cycling route – e-bikes are also available. Along with Zoom, and the equally reputable Niagara Wine Tours International (92 Picton Street), plenty of tour outfitters offer wine-cycling tours, too.

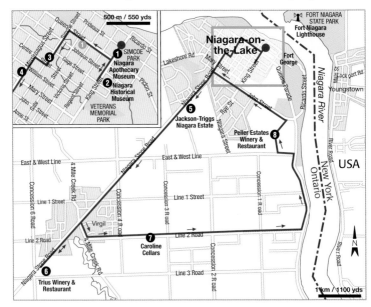

Grapes ready for harvest   *Wine tasting*

The benefit of this is that they will pre-arrange all your tastings for you (see Points to Note), and often provide a complimentary pick up of the bottles you buy.

Jackson-Triggs Niagara Estate

From town, it's an easy 5-minute (1.4km/ 0.8 mile) bike ride south along Niagara Stone Road to reach the first port of call, on your left.

A winery with an open-air theatre on-site, **Jackson-Triggs** ❺ invites you to leave your bike on the rack and enjoy yourself. Open year-round, walk-ins are welcome based on seating capacity. The patio tables make a good spot for lunch, to line your stomach for the rest of the tastings.

Trius Winery

Push on in the same direction for 5km/3 miles (around 17mins) to reach your next stop, **Trius** ❻. This lavish set-up is landscaped to perfection, down to its pink flower wall with the sign, "rosé all day". Its ice wine receives rave reviews, but it's most famous for the Trius Red, which was the first Canadian vintage to be recognised as the Best Red Wine in the World.

Caroline Cellars

Pedal back the way you came on Niagara Stone Road, and turn right at the crossroads along Four Mile Creek Road, then take a left onto Line 2 Road (3.6km/2.2 miles/around 12mins). This sedate residential street eventually peters out into vineyards, and **Caroline Cellars** ❼ will appear on your left. The Farmhouse Café

menu includes a great charcuterie, while the wine boutique has a tasting bar.

Peller

The cycle route is a delightful ride up the riverside Niagara Parkway Recreational Trail, heading north (left as you exit Riverview Cellars) for 5km/3 miles/around 16mins. Take the road to your left when you reach the parking lot and you'll see Peller's grand driveway on your right.

One of the most beautiful vineyards in Ontario, **Peller** ❽ has the elegant look of a traditional chateau. It serves ice wine in its own frozen bar, where almost everything is made out of ice – parkas are provided. Every weekend from November to March, it hosts a winter event.

To return to town, take the opposite road out of the estate to the one you entered on, turn left at the main road, and you'll be on your way back towards the town (2.7km/3 miles/around 9mins), ending the loop and just leaving you to return your bike.

Food and drink

❶ TREADWELL

114 Queen Street; www.treadwellcuisine. com; Mon–Sat 11am–2.15pm & 5–11pm, Sun 11.30am–2.15pm & 5–11pm; $$$ Feast on farm-to-fork cuisine, from roasted red pepper soup to pork belly with smoked apple to halibut with smoked Ontario heirloom risotto.

TORONTO

On the shore of Lake Ontario, six million people share what must surely be one of North America's most likeable, liveable cities. Get a flavour of its eclectic food and art scenes in between some of the major sights.

DISTANCE: 6.5km (4 miles)
TIME: A leisurely full day
START: CN Tower
END: Distillery District
POINTS TO NOTE: This route involves taking the subway. To board the TTC (Toronto Transit Commission) you must have topped up your PRESTO card or bought a PRESTO ticket from a station vending machine (single fare $3.25). There's around one-and-a-half hours of walking here. If you prefer, Toronto's streetcar and bus systems make it easy to jump between attractions (download CityMapper Toronto for live timetables). Plenty of cafés line the route, should you need a sudden respite from the Ontarian elements.

In a city where half the residents were born outside of Canada, it's practically impossible for Toronto to stagnate. Indeed, the cultural and economic centre of English-speaking Canada delivers outstanding displays of creativity and an ever-growing crop of international cafés and restaurants. Among the old-and-new architecture, the eclectic neighbourhoods and regeneration projects inhabit their own unique characters.

Toronto's sights illustrate different facets of the city, but in no way do they crystallize its identity. It remains opaque, too big and diverse to allow for a defining personality, and this adds an enticing air of excitement and unpredictability of the place.

Neither is its layout predictable: Toronto may have evolved from a lakeside settlement, but its growth has been sporadic and mostly unplanned, resulting in a cityscape that can seem a particularly random mix of the old and the new. This apparent disarray, when combined with the city's muggy summers, means most visitors spend their time hopping from sight to sight on the transit lines rather than walking. Yet, if you've the time and determination to get under the skin of the city, take to your feet and Toronto will slowly reveal itself.

Toronto skyline

CN TOWER

At 553 metres (1,815ft) – the world's tallest freestanding structure until 2010 – it's impossible to miss the slender form of the cloud-scraping **CN Tower ❶** (301 Front Street West; daily 8.30am–11pm, sometimes later) poking above the skyline. From the foot of the tower, glass-fronted elevators whisk you up the outside of the building to the indoor and outdoor Look Out Level at 346 metres (1,135ft). The circular galleries here provide panoramic views over the city and out across Lake Ontario. Details of its construction are provided in a series of photographs on the mezzanine level. The background information is extremely interesting, revealing all sorts of odd facts and figures.

If it's exhilaration you're looking for, the EdgeWalk, available in high season for a much larger charge, allows you to walk along the rim of the restaurant's roof "hands-free" 356 metres (1,167ft) above the pavement, tethered to a track above.

Upon exiting the tower, start this route by crossing over the railway pedestrian crossing, which slopes into Downtown. Bear north, picking up Blue Jays Way towards your left, and then turn left onto Richmond Street West (a 15min walk)

401 Richmond
A former tin lithography factory just south of Chinatown, **401 Richmond ❷** (Spadina Avenue and Richmond Street West; www.401richmond.com; Mon–Fri 9am–7pm, Sat 9am–6pm) has become the model of an urban art space, with thriving art galleries and affordable studios for working artists, filmmakers, architects, fashion designers, milliners and more. Here, Toronto's vibrant contemporary art scene is all under one roof.

The art hub is crowned by a relaxing leafy rooftop garden. Take a gallery guide upon arrival and browse the art and photography, including at the Abbozzo Gallery, which showcases more than 25 local and international artists.

Graffiti Alley
The modern art theme continues on an alleyway around the corner from 401. Walk left onto Spadina Avenue and go north for half a block. On your left, running parallel south of Queen Street for three blocks between Spadina and Portland avenues, is Toronto's **Graffiti Alley ❸**. A designated space for graffiti, you may get to see some Toronto's best street artists at work – and the nature of the medium means the alley might look different every time you come.

Once you've reached the end, backtrack on yourself and take the next left, up McDougall Lane. Walking from here until you rejoin Spadina Avenue, you'll pass several more impressive murals on the sides of the brick buildings.

CHINATOWN

Turning left onto Spadina Avenue brings you to Toronto's **Chinatown ❹**, one of

Graffitied car at Kensington Market

the biggest in North America, crowded with busy restaurants and stores selling everything from porcelain and jade to herbs and pickled seaweed.

The first Chinese to migrate to Canada arrived in the mid-19th century to work in BC's goldfields. Subsequently, a portion of this population migrated east, and a sizeable Chinese community sprang up in Toronto in the early 1900s. Several more waves of migration over the years have brought the population to approximately 300,000.

While you're here, it would be criminal not to try the incredible array of Asian cuisine, exemplified by **House of Gourmet**, see ➊, which has an eccentric menu of some 450 items.

Kensington Market

Dive left down Dundas Street and then right onto Kensington Avenue for the

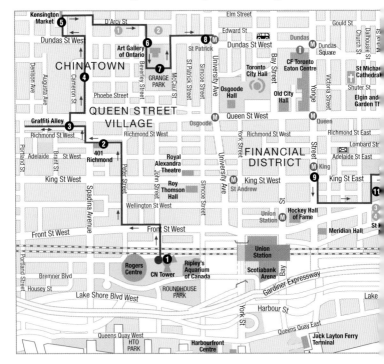

Preparing dim sum in a Chinese restaurant

pocket-sized **Kensington Market** ⑤ neighbourhood, one of the city's most bohemian enclaves. Spend a few minutes meandering around its prayer flag-strung houses and vintage boutiques.

Among Toronto's most ethnically diverse neighbourhoods, it was here, at the beginning of the 20th century, that Jewish Eastern European immigrants squeezed into a patchwork of the modest brick-and-timber houses that survive to this day. On Kensington Avenue they established a lively open-air street market, and though the market proper is no longer here, successive waves of immigrants from the Middle East, Caribbean and Asia have contributed to a lively hotchpotch of storefronts and shops. Purveyors of secondhand clothes can be found in the lower section of the neighbourhood, just off Dundas Street, while the upper part has an abundance of cafés and fresh-food stalls of every ethnic stripe.

ART GALLERY OF ONTARIO

Begin to walk back down Spadina Avenue and turn left on to D'Arcy Street and right onto Beverley Street. At the corner of Dundas Street, you will immediately see the **Art Gallery of Ontario** ⑥ (317 Dundas Street West, at Beverley; www.ago.ne; Tue and Thu 10.30am–5pm, Wed and Fri 10:30am–9pm, Sat and Sun 10.30am–5.30pm; free Wed 6–9pm). Unmissable with its startling glass-and-wood north façade, its modern transformation is thanks to Canadian-American architect Frank Gehry.

Inside, Level 1 is largely devoted to European art; Level 2 holds a wonderful collection of Canadian paintings (including *West Wind* by Tom Thomson, an iconic rendering of the northern wilderness that is perhaps the most famous of all Canadian paintings), as well as The Henry Moore Sculpture Centre. Level 3 offers the Galleria Italia, a soaring,

Park life by the Art Gallery of Ontario

airy, gallery-linking wood-and-glass hall which hosts sculpture exhibits (and an espresso bar); Level 4 has a regularly rotated selection of contemporary art, as does Level 5. There is a café, a restaurant, a large gift- and bookshop, and a first-rate programme of guided tours, free with admission.

Grange Park

Exit the gallery back onto Dundas Street West and refuel with coffee from **Art Square Café**, see ②, opposite the main entrance. Facing away from the gallery, walk to your left, then take a left turn onto Beverley Street and **Grange Park** ⑦. It features paving stones inscribed with quotes by local authors and musicians. It's also great for kids, with an adventure playground and fountains in the summer. Next to the playground, check out the **Ontario College of Art and Design**, Canada's leading design university – the building is more like a sculpture of a UFO on multicoloured stilts.

Catch the subway at **St Patrick station** ⑧ and ride it four stops to King (taking the yellow Yonge-University line towards to Finch Station). Exiting **King station** ⑨, walk south on Yonge Street and take turn left onto Wellington Street East.

FLATIRON BUILDING

At the far end of Berczy Park, on your right, you will see the **Flatiron Building**. Officially the Gooderham Build-

ing, having been built for the distiller George Gooderham in 1892, the red-brick building got its nickname thanks to its squashed shape to fit its corner plot. What really made it famous though, is the grand-scale, trompe l'oeil mural that makes it look like the building's facade is fluttering away.

Walk directly away from the Flatiron's skinny end, along Front Street East, and you'll enter the charming **St Lawrence** neighbourhood. As old as Toronto itself, this good-looking area was the original heart of the city and still embodies an old-fashioned community spirit.

ST LAWRENCE MARKET

Walk on for three minutes to **St Lawrence Market** ⑩ (South Market House building, 92 Front Street East, at Market; www.stlawrencemarket.com; Tue–Thu 8am–6pm, Fri 8am–7pm, Sat 5am–5pm). Housed in another Victorian red-brick, this cavernous building used to be Toronto's city hall and jail – today, it's a wonderland of fresh produce, selling everything from fish and freshly baked bread to international foodstuffs, all sorts of organic edibles and Ontario specialities.

Several of the market's highlights lie upstairs at the Front Street end of the market. Start with a couple of Glacier Bay oysters from **Mike's Fish Market**, see ③, then fill up on a fat peameal bacon bun from **Carousel Bakery**, see ④. Also check out **Olympic Cheese** for its stag-

Toronto's Flatiron Building   *At the St Lawrence Market*

gering range of international cheese. St Lawrence Market also regularly offers cooking classes at the **Market Kitchen** (www.themarketkitchen.ca).

Exiting the market onto Front Street East, cross the road and walk through **Market Lane Park** ⑪, turning right at the end to marvel at the palatial **St Lawrence Hall** (157 King Street East), probably Toronto's star Victorian building.

The hall was built with oodles of space for balls, public lectures and concerts; it also became the city's main meeting place for big events like the anti-slavery rallies of the 1850s. The bad taste award goes to the American showman and circus proprietor P.T. Barnum. It was here in St Lawrence Hall (among other spots) where Barnum saw the potential of the diminutive (60cm/23-inch) Charles Sherwood Stratton, aka Tom Thumb, exhibiting him as a curiosity to stump up a few dollars.

DISTILLERY DISTRICT

Drop back down to Front Street East and then take a right onto Trinity Street (a 16-minute walk), to reach the **Distillery District** ⑫ (55 Mill Street, near the foot of Parliament Street; www.thedistillery-district.com). This is the city's most diverse arts complex, sited in a capacious former distillery, which forms an appealing industrial "village" on Mill Street. You can get here on the King streetcar #504 east (from the same side of the street as St Lawrence Hall) to Parliament Street,

from where it's a five minute walk.

The Distillery District started life as the Gooderham and Worts Distillery, a rambling network of over 40 brick buildings that constituted the largest distillery in the British Empire. In operation until 1990, the distillery was founded in 1832, when ships could sail into its own jetty.

Since its demise, the distillery has been sympathetically redeveloped by a small group of entrepreneurs, who chose to integrate many of the original features into the revamp – including its quirky walkways and bottle runways – and to exclude all multinational chains. One of the architectural highlights is the Pure Spirits building, which features French doors and a fancy wrought-iron balcony.

With hand-made-jewellery stores, crafts and fashion designers, it's best to simply browse the shops and see what catches your eye. Be sure to visit the artisan chocolate factory and **SOMA** (32 Tank House Lane) for gifts.

The arts

Two highly rated galleries are on Distillery Lane, the **Arta** at number 14 and the **Thompson Landry** at number 32. Also check out the **steel arachnid** installation, created by Oakland artist Michael Christian.

Among performance venues is the **Soulpepper theatre** (50 Tank House Lane; www.soulpepper.ca), selling affordable tickets to their progressive plays (and free to under 25s for selected performances).

Distillery District

Food and drink

There's an array of international cuisine to be enjoyed around here, but Italian **Archeo**, see ⑤, is the chicest restaurant space in the district. After, pull up a stool at **The Beer Hall** opposite SOMA, see ⑥, which frequently wins awards for its huge craft beer selection.

Got a taste for beer? Stay another day and book a tour with Beer Lover's Tours (tel: 416 662 6312; www.beer loverstour.com; Union Station to Eglinton Subway Station). The company's all-day Saturday beer tours are a Toronto staple, and include a charcuterie lunch; for an additional $50, you can add on a four-course "beer dinner".

Food and drink

① HOUSE OF GOURMET

484 Dundas Street West; www.houseof gourmet.blogspot.com; daily 10am–midnight $
It's especially coveted for its wonton-brisket-noodle-soup and steamed rice rolls, but there's something to suit everyone on the huge menu of Cantonese cuisine. Brisk service and a casual atmosphere make it a perfect lunch spot.

② ART SQUARE CAFÉ

334 Dundas Street West; www.artsquare cafe.com; daily 9am–11pm; $$
In a sandy-brick building fronted by iron railings, this cosy space does good coffee, as well as cakes, crepes and pastries to eat in or take away.

③ MIKE'S FISH MARKET

93 Front Street East; www.stlawrencemarket.com; Mon–Sat; $
The oyster bar at Mike's seafood stall offers a variety of oyster species and an assortment of condiments to spice things up.

④ CAROUSEL BAKERY

93 Front Street East; www.stlawrencemarket.com; Tue–Sat; $
St Lawrence Market has a bunch of choice vendors, but Carousel is noted as the top place to try Toronto's famed peameal bacon sandwich and a butter tart.

⑤ ARCHEO

31 Trinity Street; Mon–Fri 5–9pm, Sat–Sun noon–9pm; $$
High ceilings and exposed brick walls bring modern flair to Archeo's seasonally changing, Italian comfort-food menu. Frequently closes for events though, so call ahead.

⑥ THE BEER HALL

21 Tank House Lane; daily 2–9pm; tel: 416 681 0338; $$
Connected to the Mill Street Brew Pub, this microbrewery offers an ever-changing roster of small batch beer made on-site. Order a flight that includes the excellent Tankhouse Organic Ale.

Churchill's northern lights

THOMPSON TO CHURCHILL, MANITOBA

Take the train from Thompson to this Hudson Bay outpost (16-hour overnight train) to see beluga whales or polar bears up-close. This northern town bills itself as the "polar bear capital of the world" with justification.

DISTANCE: 520km (323 miles)
TIME: 3 days
START/END: Thompson
POINTS TO NOTE: Book the elements of this trip swiftly: transportation, accommodation and tundra buggy tours are usually non-refundable and you don't want to be stuck with a reservation without everything in place. You'll need insulated clothing too, including footwear suitable for -40C. Churchill is well beyond the reach of Manitoba's highways, but connected by train, with VIA Rail (www.viarail.ca) running services to Thompson (3 weekly), The Pas (2 weekly) and Winnipeg (2 weekly). You can also fly from Winnipeg. North Frontier Adventures operators run charter flights from Montreal and Calgary.

On the east bank of the Churchill River where it empties into Hudson Bay, Churchill has a rickety, unassuming look – but its incredibly accessible opportunities to view the wildlife that moves through it make this a once-in-a-lifetime destination. Being so difficult to reach only makes it feel like more of a diversion from reality for those who make it here.

THOMPSON

This route begins in **Thompson ❶**, a sprawling nickel-mining town at the end of Hwy-6 and 399km (248 miles) from The Pas – as far north as you can go on Manitoba's network of sealed highways and a long-haul journey in itself.

Driving to Thompson, you'll pass through hundreds of kilometres of boreal forest, with barely another vehicle in sight – but from here you can to take the overnight train to Churchill, thereby cutting the cost and journey time of picking up the service in Winnipeg.

Thompson's Visitor Information Centre incorporates the **Heritage North Museum** (charge), which bursts with stuffed local wildlife and history. They can also organize tours of local mines and suggest other ways in which to kill a few hours before your train leaves, if you're not busy stocking up on groceries in the large downtown malls.

Welcome to Churchill

Food and accommodation

While you wait for your train, grab a bite at **Pub55**, see ❶. If you need to spend the night, the only hotel in town is **Best Western Thompson Hotel**, see page 109, which also has a gastropub. You can leave your car at City Hall, almost opposite at 226 Mystery Lake Road, while you take on your rail journey north.

Train to Churchill

Thompson's **train station** ❷ is just southeast of the town centre – take Station Road, just south of Wal-Mart. The overnight train leaves for Churchill (three weekly) and takes 16 hours – so get comfy. One-way tickets through VIA Rail are relatively cheap for a standard reclining seat, or there's an option to fork out a handsome sum for a sleeper cabin. Breakfast, lunch and dinner are served on every journey and there's an on-board snack bar. Plus, just outside each restroom you'll find a tap to refill drinking-water bottles.

CHURCHILL

Alight the train and **pop into the Parks Canada Visitor Center** ❸, within the station, to learn about the region's Indigenous culture, historic sites and modern way of life. More useful before you go is Travel Manitoba's dedicated website: www.everythingchurchill.com.

Step out onto the road named Mantayo Seepee Mescanow and the town is in front of you, a finger of land pointing into the wide river. Churchill's centre is compact – it takes a mere 10 minutes to walk from one end to the other.

Flanking the train station and adjacent Parks Canada Visitor Centre, **Kelsey Boulevard** is the town's main street. **Tamarak Rentals**, a 10-minute walk to your right along Kelsey Boulevard, rents out SUVs, which can be useful if you are here primarily for the Northern Lights and want to take off at any time of day.

Hotel

The polar bear presence means you can't camp in Churchill, but otherwise the town's reasonable range of accommodation is an easy walk from the train station and should be reserved in advance, even outside peak bear season when the prices double. There are good-value rooms at the **Seaport Hotel** (215 Kelsey Boulevard), see page 109. As its dining rooms are open 7am to 10pm all year round, it's a great place to refresh and recoup no matter what time of day you arrive, see ❷.

Pop into the **Arctic Trading Company** to browse local handicrafts and buy any extra clothing for your stay, such as moccasins, mukluks and mittens.

The Beluga

A left on Kelsey Boulevard and then any right will bring you to the snow-dusted coast, including a rock stack in homage to the ancient Inuit inuksuk practice. Adjacent to the Town Complex (the long, flat, brown building) is the remains of **The Beluga** ❹, a fishing boat that's been

Beluga whale   *Miss Piggy plane wreck*

converted into a space to sit and look out to Hudson Bay. Churchill is one of Canada's best Northern Lights destinations – the beach here is a great place to look out for the auroras. It is visible throughout the year, but is most spectacular January through March.

Itsanitaq Museum
Tucked to the side of the Town Complex is the small **Itsanitaq Museum ❺**, pre-viously the Eskimo Museum, (Tue–Sat 9am–5pm, Mon 1–5pm; donation). A visit here will shed light on Inuit culture and its 4,000-year history; the taxidermy walrus and polar bears give you an up-close look at the impressive beasts.

Plane wreck
East of the town, about an eight-minute drive, is the intriguing site dubbed **Miss Piggy plane wreck ❻**, in a space so rocky

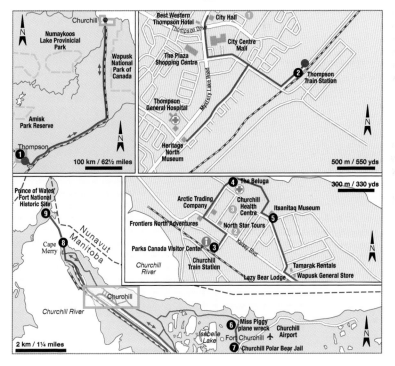

Polar bears

and remote it looks like it simply dropped out of the sky. The Curtiss C-46 freight crashed here in 1979, amazingly without a single fatality. The name came about because it once carried a cargo of pigs.

Polar bear jail

When a polar bear gets a little too relaxed around town, they are tranquilized and sent to the **Churchill Polar Bear Jail ⑦**. This facility is a safe place for them to be held before the ice refreezes enough for them to be on their way. You can't go in, but it's worth a look for the giant polar bear painted onto the side of the "jail."

Tours

Even if you choose to rent a vehicle, it's likely you'll want to arrange a tour or experience for some point of your trip. **North Star Tours** (Bayport Plaza, Munck Street; www.northstartours.net) is a good first stop to get a feel for what's on offer at any time of year. The company is headed up by a jolly third-generation local who runs an excellent minibus tour of local sites – which includes a good look for polar bears – but they won't hesitate to suggest, and even call, other companies for you if you have particular activities in mind.

Aside from wildlife-watching, there are a couple of sights, slightly out of town, where it would be useful to have a local drive you there if you haven't got your own vehicle. Taxi drivers are also usually more than willing to double up as guides.

Cape Merry

Swinging right around to the western tip (23-minute drive), **Cape Merry ⑧** has the remains of an 18th-century gun emplacement and a cairn commemorating Danish explorer Jens Munck, who led an expedition forced to winter here in 1619; most of the crew died from cold and hunger.

At high tide the cape is a great spot from which to watch belugas in the bay. It's an atmospheric 30-minute walk from town – but as a polar bear hangout, it's dangerous here without a guide.

Prince of Wales Fort

On the opposite side of the estuary from Cape Merry, **Prince of Wales' Fort National Historic Site ⑨** (July and Aug; only accessible as part of a $115 guided tour of the Churchill River by Sea North Tours) is a partly restored 18th-century stone fortress built to protect the interests of the Hudson's Bay Company from the French. Finished in 1771, this massive structure took 40 years to complete.

POLAR BEARS

Of course, the reason most people make this long journey is for the wildlife. Polar bears start to arrive in June, forced ashore until the ice re-forms enough to support their weight, allowing them to hunt seals; a polar bear can detect a scent from 32km (20 miles) away and can pick up the presence of seals under a metre of snow and ice.

A traditional stone inukshuk

In October and November, just before the ice re-forms completely, you are pretty much guaranteed to see polar bears. Some tour outfits have specialist backcountry tundra buggies, to get you access to the hard-to-reach places (although you pay handsomely for these excursions). **Frontiers North Adventures** (140 Kelsey Boulevard) offer a full day, lasting between six and eight hours.

After a long day bear-spotting, warm up over dinner at the **Tundra Inn**, see ➌.

Beluga whales

In June the Churchill River ice begins to break, creating a spreading patch of open water that attracts up to 3,000 white beluga whales. These intelligent, inquisitive and vocal mammals spend July and August around the mouth of the river, joining the seals, who arrive in late March for five months.

Summer brings more than 3,000 beluga whales to the mouth of the Churchill River to feed. If you are here in July and August, join **Sea North Tours** for a beluga whale kayak experience or SUP (both 3 hours), on the Churchill River.

You'll feel as if you are one of the pod being this close to the water, which is teeming with the ethereal-looking white whales. Arrive 30 minutes before the posted tour time at their office at 153 Kelsey Boulevard.

Dog-sleds

Seen the bears and belugas? Try dog sledding with Indigenous-run Wapusk Adven-

tures, which departs daily from **Wapusk General Store** (321 Kelsey Boulevard; www.wapuskadventures.com). They scoot you to their dog camp located 6.4km (4 miles) from Churchill. You'll be met by 28 eager staff members, at least one of whom is a human.

The overnight train back to Thompson usually sets off on the 260km (160-mile) journey from Churchill at 7.30pm, so you can easily fit an excursion in.

Food and drink

➊ PUB55
73 Commercial Place, Thompson; 11am–1am; www.pub55.com; $$
A wings, ribs and burgers place with a relaxed atmosphere and an outdoor seating area. There's also a pool table for those with some time to spare.

➋ SEAPORT HOTEL
215 Kelsey Boulevard, Churchill; 7am–10pm; www.seaporthotel.ca; $$
A key locals' hangout, this casual diner and pub attached to the hotel shows sports on TV and occasionally hosts live music.

➌ TUNDRA INN
34 Franklin Street; Tue–Sat 4pm–9pm; www.tundrainn.com; $$$
There's frequent live entertainment in this bustling pub, which serves hearty Arctic-inspired food, such as bison burger. It's family-friendly too.

SASKATCHEWAN'S SOUTHWEST

The Prairies between Ontario and the Rocky Mountains are often overlooked, but a day's worth of driving through Saskatchewan will take you to two richly rewarding landscapes, the Cypress Hills and Great Sands dunes, with Western history in between.

DISTANCE: 380km (236 miles)
TIME: 1.5 days
START: Historic Reesor Ranch
END: Great Sand Hills
POINTS TO NOTE: There is no reason why this route can't be done in the winter, when ranch horse-riding becomes skidooing and hiking is swapped for cross-country skiing (although the small museums close). However, you'll need a 4WD/AWD, heavy-duty snow tires, and the essential winter driving precautions.

Spreading over the provinces of Manitoba, Saskatchewan and Alberta, the vast lands commonly called "the Prairies" don't tend to pull in the visitors like their dramatic Rockies neighbours. In these parts, isolated farms guard thousands of acres of swaying wheat or immense grasslands with giant herds of cattle.

However, straddling the Saskatchewan–Alberta border, the wooded ridges of the Cypress Hills rise above the plains in a 130km (80-mile) -long plateau that in places reaches a height of 1,400 metres (4,593ft) – the highest point in Canada between Labrador and the Rockies. Its wetter and milder climate has created a lush environment that supports a wealth of wildlife, including elk, lynx, bobcat and coyote.

Beyond the verdant forested valleys, Saskatchewan has a clutch of national parks and intriguing landscapes, such as the Great Sand Hills, a 1,900-sq-km (734-sq-mile) area of active desert-like sand dunes. All the while, as you drive between the towns, you'll start to get into the Western spirit by learning the history of the Mounties, whisky hustlers and cowboys of the Prairies' past.

HISTORIC REESOR RANCH

Historic Reesor Ranch ❶ (Box 1001; Maple Creek; www.reesorranch.com) makes a great launchpad for setting off into Saskatchewan. It embodies the spirit of Canada's Prairies, having been established by pioneer ranchers in 1904. Horseback activities include trekking through the forests and grasslands

of the Cypress Hills, and cattle-herding, the old-fashioned wranglers' way. It's a good place to stay the night, not least because Cypress Hills' Dark Sky Preserve-status means constellation-spotting here is at a whole new level.

FORT WALSH NATIONAL HISTORIC PARK

The exit for the ranch spits you out on the Alberta side of Cypress Hills. Take a left at the junction, and Battle Creek Road will lead you back around into Saskatchewan.

After 25 minutes you will reach **Fort Walsh National Historic Park ❷** (www. parkscanada.ca/walsh; July–Aug daily 9.30am–5pm, May, June and Sept Tue–Sat 9.30am–5pm). From 1878 to 1882 the fort served as the headquarters of the North West Mounted Police, the "Mounties," who'd trammel these parts on horseback as they were tasked with bringing law and order to the Wild West.

A five-minute walk behind the park's information centre, and accessed from the eastern entrance to the park by the increasingly bumpy Hwy-271, there are excellent displays on the Plains Indians, fort history and the development of the RCMP. The officers' quarters, commissioner's residence, and various other buildings have all been recreated.

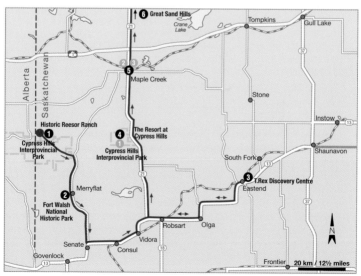

Bull moose in the Cypress Hills

Guides in period costume take you on a tour of whitewashed log buildings, the whole site having been restored.

Battle Creek

Every 45 minutes a minibus makes the trip from the information centre over the hills to **Battle Creek**, where Abel Farwell's whisky trading post has been reconstructed to commemorate the 1873 Cypress Hills Massacre. The guides will take you to the site of the massacre itself: a violent confrontation between a group of white wolf-hunters, whisky traders and a band of Assiniboine, that left 70 dead.

T.Rex Discovery Centre

Travel somewhat further back into Saskatchewan's history with a look at its prehistoric finds, by driving on to the town of Eastend on Highway 615, then 13 (The Red Coat Trail), for 90 minutes (110km/68 miles).

Sitting incongruously in the plains is a sleek state-of-the-art facility containing the **T.Rex Discovery Centre ❸**, so remote it gets its own address (1 T-Rex Drive, Eastend; daily 10am–6pm; donation). On display are the area's astounding fossils – including a complete Tyrannosaurus Rex skeleton found near here by a local high school teacher in 1991. There are tours throughout the day and a visit to an active quarry may be possible.

This site is not en-route, so backtrack the way you came for half an hour until you reach the turnoff for Highway 21, where you start to head north.

The Resort at Cypress Hills

Take a break at **The Resort at Cypress Hills ❹** (Box 1480, Maple Creek, Saskatchewan; www.resortatcypresshills.ca), left along the turnoff of Highway 221 and an hour in total from T. Rex, where you can buy refreshments at **Ivan's Restaurant**, see ❶.

Cypress Hills has been separated into two sections, Centre Block and West Block, with the West sprawling to the Alberta border and Fort Walsh. The larger, more untamed West is broken up by steep hills and deep, sheltered ravines, while the highly accessible Centre Block has abundant facilities, such as this Resort, with its five campgrounds, marked trails and water activities on Loch Leven.

Maple Creek

Push up north to the first "Cow Town" of the old West, **Maple Creek ❺**, 25 minutes (33km/20.5 miles) from the Resort. This is ranching country, about as Old West as Saskatchewan gets, and its streets are full of pick-up trucks, cowboy boots and Stetsons. It is also the market town for a number of Hutterite colonies (the only prairie community to have maintained its communal ideal), whose women stand out with their floral dresses and headscarves.

A good place to eat here is **Jimmy's Kitchen**, see ❷, slightly north of the town centre. You could also grab some bottles-to-go from the town's own brewery, **Rafter R Brewing**, see ❸.

Everything reaches wild heights in late September during Maple Creek's Cowboy

Fort Walsh cemetery

Fort Walsh buldings and wagon

Poetry Gathering, a literary celebration of wranglers that draws cowboys from across North America. Some of the late 19th-century brick storefronts have survived, and the tidy **Oldtimers' Museum** (222 Jasper Street; May–Sept Tue–Sat 9am–5.30pm; donation), has good displays on pioneer life and the Mounties.

GREAT SAND HILLS

From Maple Creek, drive another 100km/ 62 miles (1 hour 20 minutes) north up Highway 21, to the village of **Liebenthal**. This is the best place to view the vast area of giant sand dunes, where kangaroo rats hop and mule deer and antelope graze, known as the **Great Sand Hills 6**.

However, the place to access them is the village of **Sceptre**, around 18km (11 miles) north of the dunes. To reach it, continue driving north and turn right at Highway 32. After around half an hour, Sceptre will be on your right. Here, the small **Great Sand Hills Museum** (www.greatsandhillsmuseum.com; mid-May to early Sept Mon–Sun 10am–noon and 12.30–4.30pm, Sun 1–5pm) has displays on the ecology of the hills and provides printed directions for exploring the dunes.

From Sceptre, take the grid road on the east side of the village (off Highway 32) for 9.6km (6 miles), follow the curve to the right at the T junction, travel west for 1.6km (1 mile), then south for approximately 10km (6.2 miles) to the parking lot with interpretive signs. Then you walk 0.5km (0.3 mile) on a narrow sandy trail to the dune formations.

You may want to bring snowshoes for walking on the shape-shifting sand; or, for a faster thrill, take one of the toboggans and sail down the slope 500 metres (1,640 feet) away.

Food and drink

① IVAN'S RESTAURANT

5 Pine Avenue, Cypress Hills Interprovincial Park, Maple Creek; www.resortatcypresshills.ca/dining; $$
The only all-season restaurant within the park, its fried breakfasts will set you up for a day in the snow. It does food-to-go as well as seated service in a chalet-style dining room.

② JIMMY'S KITCHEN

21 Hwy N; daily 11.30am–9pm; www.jimmyskitchen.business.site; $
Maple Creek is a town that's big on burgers, pizza and fried chicken and short on variety. This does what it does well.

③ RAFTER R BREWING

13 Pacific Avenue, Maple Creek; Tue–Sat; www.rafterrbrewing.ca; $$
A newish brewery offering exciting seasonal beers in a cool, minimal space. Non-alcoholic beer is also available. No food is served but you're welcome to bring your own or order delivery from one of the town's restaurants.

Black bear cub

ICEFIELDS PARKWAY, ALBERTA

*Cutting through the heart of the Rockies, the splendour of the Icefields Parkway
(Hwy-93), stretching north from Lake Louise, can hardly be overstated.
This section of it can be done as a day-trip or as part of a longer road trip.*

DISTANCE: 130km (81 miles) plus hikes

TIME: One day

START: Lake Louise Village

END: Columbia Icefield

POINTS TO NOTE: A free pamphlet from Parks Canada visitor centres provides a detailed map and summary of all sights and trailheads, and bus tours along the route are available. Do this route in September or October for glorious fall colours. There is no public transport on this route but guided bus tours are available, see Brewster Sightseeing (www.banffjaspercollection.com). This being bear territory, always carry bear spray. Make noise as you walk, especially when approaching blind corners and through shrubby areas.

Frequently ranked as one of the world's best drives, the Icefields Parkway's unending succession of huge peaks, immense glaciers, iridescent lakes, wildflower meadows, wildlife and forests – capped by the stark grandeur of the Columbia Icefield – can be almost overwhelming. The drive itself is enough to evoke a sense of adventure, but take your time to explore the panoply of trails, viewpoints and the chance to soak up the incredible scenery.

The Icefield Parkway is a is a 232km (144-mile) double-lane highway linking Jasper and Lake Louise. This 130km (81-mile) section of the route takes 1hr 40 minutes, but you can take as long as you like exploring the trails along the way.

LAKE LOUISE

Lake Louise Village ❶ might not amount to much, but it's a practical place to begin the route, as an essential supply stop, with more or less everything you need in terms of food, accommodation, information and equipment rental. Grab a coffee at **Bill Peyto's Café**, see ❶, and lunch for later if you'd prefer to eat on the go.

Drive to the lake, 4.5km (2.8 miles) away (and 200 metres/656ft higher), on the winding Lake Louise Drive. Before you see Lake Louise you see the **Fairmont Château Lake Louise**, a grandiose mon-

Peyto Lake

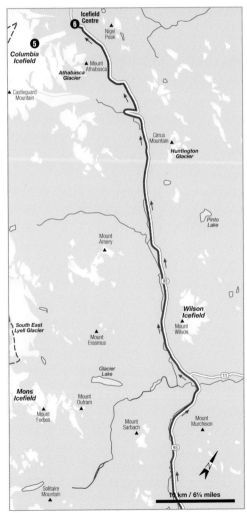

strosity, though it fades into insignificance beside the immense beauty of its surroundings.

Lakeshore Walk

The lake is brilliant turquoise, the mountains sheer, the glaciers vast; the whole ensemble is perfection. And you don't even have to break into a sweat to take it all in. The easy **Lakeshore Walk ❷** gets you up-close to the azure waters, and leaves you with energy for more hiking later in the day (it is also wheelchair and pushchair-accessible). It's 4.5km (2.8 miles) there and back along the northern shore (about an hour in total). Set off early, when the trail is much quieter. In summer you can also rent canoes from this shoreline.

Highway 93/ Icefields Parkway

Head back toward the village on Lake Louise Drive, but shoot off to the left on the Trans-Canada Highway (road 93), which becomes the Icefields Parkway at this point.

Lake Louise

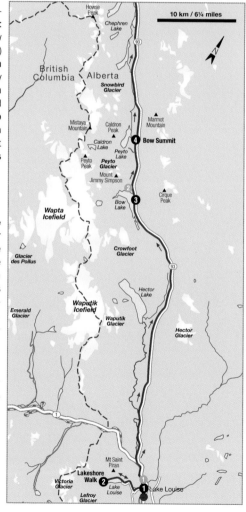

For non-drivers, Brewster Transportation (tel: 403 762 6710; www.brewstertransportation.com) runs several tours and a single scheduled bus daily in both directions between Banff, Lake Louise and Jasper from late May to mid-October. A word with the driver will usually get you dropped off at hostels and trailheads en route.

Bow Lake and Bow Glacier Falls

The first stop is **Bow Lake** ❸, and another chance for hiking. You'll see the lake on your left and then the turn for the car park soon after. A great short trail sets off from beside the Simpson's Num-Ti-Jah Lodge, to Bow Lake and Bow Glacier Falls (4.3km/2.7 miles; 155 metre/508ft ascent; 1–2hr one way), taking in the flats around Bow Lake – one of the Rockies' most beautiful – and climbing to some immense cliffs and several waterfalls beyond. Back at Simpson's Num-Ti-Jah Lodge – one of the most famous in the Rockies – have lunch at its **Elkhorn Dining Room**, see ❷.

Elk   *Bow Glacier Falls*

BOW SUMMIT AND PEYTO LAKE

The highest point crossed by any Canadian highway comes around 5km (3 miles) further up the road: the 2,069-metre (6,788ft) pass at **Bow Summit** ❹, source of the Bow River, the waterway that flows through Banff, Lake Louise and Calgary.

Just beyond is the unmissable twenty-minute stroll to **Peyto Lake Viewpoint** (1.4km/0.8 mile; 100 metres/328ft), one of the finest vistas in the Rockies. The beautiful panorama only unfolds in the last seconds, giving a stunning view of the vivid emerald lake far below; mountains and forest stretch away as far as you can see.

COLUMBIA ICEFIELD

Just beyond Sunwapta Pass (133km/82.6 miles from Lake Louise) and covering an area of 325 sq km (125 sq miles), the **Columbia Icefield** ❺ is the largest collection of ice and snow in the Rockies, and the biggest glacial area in the northern hemisphere outside the Arctic Circle.

It's also the most accessible of some 17 glacial areas along the Parkway. Meltwater flows from the Icefield into the Arctic, Atlantic and Pacific oceans, forming a so-called "hydrological apex" – the only other one in the world is in Siberia. This is fed by six major glaciers.

Icefield Centre and the Glacier Skywalk
The busy **Icefield Centre** ❻ (daily May to Sept 9am–5pm; free Glacier Skywalk daily: Late Apr, May and Sept 10am–5pm;

June–early Aug 9am–6pm; early Aug–early Sept 9am–7pm; Oct 10am–4pm) embellishes the background information and sheds light on both the Columbia Icefield and Canada's most extensive cave system – the Castleguard Caves.

The centre provides a viewpoint for the most prominent part of the icefields: the Athabasca Glacier, which has substantially shrunk since the centre's construction. Its Glacier Skywalk is a horseshoe-shaped, glass-floored walkway that elevates visitors 280 metres (919ft) above the mountain goats and crashing waterfalls of the Sunwapta Valley.

Food and drink

❶ BILL PEYTO'S CAFÉ

203 Village Road; daily 7am–4pm; $$
This relaxed hostel café, open to non-guests, serves great snacks and reasonably priced full meals. The menu includes sandwiches, burgers, mountainous nachos, salads and pasta.

❷ ELKHORN DINING ROOM

Mile 22 Icefields Parkway; www.num-ti-jah.com/elkhorn-dining-room; $$$
This original hunting lodge comes complete with stone fireplace and majestic views. Dine on elk burgers or crispy steelhead trout beneath the watchful eye of moose, wolverines and other hunting trophies. Guests get seating priority; if you're staying elsewhere make sure you reserve.

VANCOUVER

With its watery, mountain-ringed setting, Vancouver is one of the world's great scenic cities. The best way to take in the Harbour's majesty is by bike, as this route does, to link up Downtown Vancouver with Stanley Park.

DISTANCE: 10.5km (6.5 miles)

TIME: 1 day

START/END: Gastown

POINTS TO NOTE: If you choose to get the bus instead of bike, you'll need exact change (single journey $3). Alternatively, buy a refillable Compass Card ($6 refundable deposit) from a station vending machine, which you can top-up online to pay for the bus, SkyTrain or SeaBus.

Cradled between the ocean and mountains, Vancouver has a dazzling Downtown district that fills a narrow peninsula bounded by Burrard Inlet to the north, English Bay to the west and False Creek to the south. You'll find a sophisticated and hedonistic city, having more in common with the West Coast ethos and outlook of San Francisco than, say, Toronto or Ottawa to the east.

Vancouver is not a city that requires relentless sightseeing – although this route covers several major sights – but it's best enjoyed by stopping regularly to soak up the views, linger over coffee and

dip in and out of bars.

GASTOWN

You'll inevitably spend a good deal of time in the Downtown area and its Victorian-era equivalent, **Gastown**, a hip stretch of boutique shops and coffee houses near the harbour's edge.

This route starts at **Maple Tree Square ❶**, the heart of Gastown and focus of its main streets. **Gastown** is a fantastic piece of city rejuvenation distinguished by cobblestone streets and 20th-century brick buildings.

The name derives from "Gassy" (as in loquacious) Jack Leighton, a retired sailor turned publican and self-proclaimed "mayor", who arrived on site by canoe in 1867, quickly opening a bar to service the nearby lumber mills – his statue stands on the square.

Walk down Water Street, where it's a Gastown rite of passage to snap photos with the **Steam Clock ❷**, on the corner of Cambie Street. Easily identified by the fog emanating from its frame, the two-tonne landmark sounds out the "Westminster

False Creek panorama

chime" every 15 minutes and was the first of its kind when built in 1977.

Two minutes' walk along Cambie Street, opposite the Steam Clock, **Revolver**, see ❶, is an excellent place to stop for coffee.

WATERFRONT

At the end of Water Street, bear left to pick up West Cordova Street, then a right up Howe Street (a 1km/0.6 mile walk from Maple Square) and you will arrive

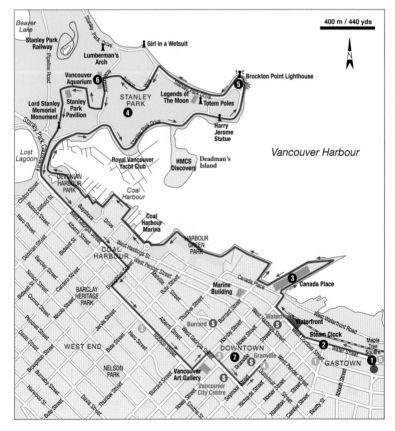

Gastown Steam Clock

at the edge of Vancouver Harbour. A stroll down here takes you past excellent public art including the pixelated **Digital Orca** from local celeb Douglas Coupland, and the Olympic Cauldron from 2010, which is lit on special occasions.

Canada Place

Also located here is **Canada Place** ❸ (Canada Place Walkways; open 24hr; free), the Canadian pavilion for Expo '86. An architectural tour de force at the time it was built, the Place houses a luxury hotel, cruise-ship terminal and a glitzy convention centre. It makes a superb viewpoint, buzzing with boats, helicopters and floatplanes, with sweeping vistas of the port and the mountains.

FlyOver Canada (www.flyovercanada. com; daily 10am–9pm) is a more recent addition to Canada Place, a popular 30-minute virtual flight experience that takes you "gliding" over the many natural and man-made marvels of Canada, complete with wind, scents and mists. Curiously exhilarating – and although the ride itself is only eight minutes long, the rest of the time being a pre-show and boarding – it's certainly worth the entry fee.

An alternative to Canada Place's vantage point, the **Harbour Centre** (555 West Hastings Street; www.vancouverlookout. com; mid-May to Sept 8.30am–10.30pm; Oct–early May 9am–9pm) is one of the city's tallest structures. On a fine day, it's worth paying to ride the stomach-churning glass elevators that run up the side of the tower – 168.6 metres (553ft) in 40 seconds – to the 40th-floor observation deck, which has a staggering 360-degree view. Admission is valid all day so you can return and look out over the bright lights of Vancouver at night.

CYCLE TO STANLEY PARK

For a taste of the city's greener side, hit Stanley Park, a huge area of semi-wild parkland, forest and beaches that crowns the northern tip of the Downtown peninsula.

The most scenic approach to Stanley Park is along the Seawall from Coal Harbour, which begins at Canada Place and parallels West Cordova Street. You can walk but, given the distance of several kilometres, it's best done on two wheels.

Bike rental couldn't be easier in Vancouver: download the app for its shared bike system, Mobi (www.mobibikes.ca), and add the unlimited 30-minute rides option. Take as many rides as you want in 24 hours, with the first 30 minutes of each ride included in the $12 price. A map will show you where to find the bikes – each one comes with a helmet attached (it's the law to wear one). Once you've picked up your bike, simply trace the waterfront northwest toward the park (which you can see across the bay).

Alternatively, take trolleybus 19 to Stanley Park ($2.75; www.translink.ca) from the corner of Burrard and Pender streets, which drops you just inside the park, a five-minute walk from the Aquarium, one of the main destinations.

Pulling in at Canada Place   *Stanley Park*

Seawall

Taking in unspoiled views of the water and mountains, the scenic Seawall is one of Vancouver's finest features. It wraps around the city's Downtown core and Stanley Park as part of the world's longest uninterrupted waterfront path, the 28km (17-mile) **Seaside Greenway**. The path is divided into two sections: the one nearest the water is for walkers and runners, and the inside path is for cyclists and inline skaters.

STANLEY PARK

One of the world's great urban spaces, **Stanley Park ❹** is Vancouver's green heart, helping lend the city its particular character. At nearly 4 sq km (1.5 sq miles), it's one of the largest urban parks in North America – a semi-wilderness of dense rainforest, marshland and three beaches: English Bay which has a waterslide during summer season; Second Beach with its pool and concession stands; and the quieter Third Beach which allows barbecues. Ocean laps the park on three sides, with Seawall all the way round. A brisk walk of this coastal path takes two to three hours and you get exceptional views of the city and across the water to the mountains.

Brockton Point

As you follow the waterfront counterclockwise around the park, an iconic view of downtown and its yachts comes into view, opening up into a panorama as you reach a Stanley Park landmark, the red-and-white **Brockton Point Lighthouse ❺**, dating from 1914.

A little further, at the pedestrian crossing, you can make a quick detour left to see the garden of **totem poles**, which marks the fact that in its former incarnation Stanley Park was the traditional territory of Coast Salish First Nations. The first poles were at Lumberman's Arch, originally from Vancouver Island's Alert Bay in the 1920s, and then more were added in 1936 from Haida Gwaii and BC's central coast Rivers inlet. In the mid-1960s, they were moved to Brockton Point, and then sent to various museums for preservation. Some of the remaining poles are loaned replacements, others specially commissioned.

Continue cycling for another minute and just after Vancouver's most famous statue, the *Girl in a Wetsuit* – a sporty twist on Copenhagen's Little Mermaid – head away from the waterfront by turning left onto Avison Way.

VANCOUVER AQUARIUM

At the end of Avison Way is **Vancouver Aquarium ❻** (www.vanaqua.org; daily 10am–5pm; seasonal hours and statutory holidays 9.30am–6pm). Leave your bikes at the Mobi bikeshare station on Avison Way and take a few hours to explore this star attraction.

Ranked among North America's best attractions of its kind, the Vancouver Aquarium is the park's most popular

Totem poles at Brockton Point in Stanley Park

destination. Home to over 50,000 animals including penguins, sea otters and beluga whales, and with state-of-the-art exhibits, a recent renovation has added a new entranceway, indoor and outdoor cafés, and a two-level exhibition space that houses large temporary exhibitions.

The Arctic section concerns the fragile world of the Canadian North, offering a chance to see belugas face-to-face through glass and peer in at cod, char, sea cucumbers and hot-pink sea anemones, all indigenous to this icy domain. The steamy Amazon gallery displays the vegetation, fish, marmosets, sloths and other creatures of the rainforest in a climate-controlled environment; while the Wild Coast habitat performs a similar role for otters, harbour porpoises and other animals of the waters of BC.

Whale-watching

From March to October, thousands of whales migrate through Vancouver's waters. Most outfits offer "guaranteed" whale sightings so if you don't see them on your first trip, you can return again for free. While there are many whale-watching tours to choose from, they offer almost identical trips at the same prices, typically around $120 for a three-hour outing. Prince of Whales (1516 Duranleau Street, Granville Island) is the most easily accessible from this route. Out of season, it also operates high-speed harbour cruises aboard a 12-passenger Zodiac.

Annually, the aquarium sees more than a million visitors. To avoid cramming in like a sardine, visit on a weekday.

Transport to downtown

Grab a bike and cycle back to Downtown, or walk 10 minutes to catch the number 19 trolleybus from **Stanley Park Loop Bay 2**. The stop is located to the west of the aquarium, walking either left or right on Avison Way to loop around. Buses arrive every seven minutes and the journey costs $2.50. Alight at **W Pender St @ Jervis St** – although any of the clustered stops on this stretch are fine.

DOWNTOWN

You soon get the hang of Vancouver's **Downtown 7** district, an arena of avenues and shopping malls centred on **Robson Street**. On hot summer evenings, it's a buzzy meeting place crammed with bars, restaurants, late-night stores, and youths sucking down Bubble Tea or eating frozen yoghurt. At other times a more sedate class hangs out on the steps of the **Vancouver Art Gallery** (750 Hornby Street), or glides in and out of the big department stores.

Food and drink

Vancouver's restaurant scene is a fast-paced delicious dazzle of new openings and chef switcheroos spread across the city. Downtown and Gastown have an ever-growing crop of culinary hot-spots and experimental cocktail bars.

Vancouver Aquarium

Meander east during your evening, to end the day at Gastown's fabulous bars. **CinCin**, see ②, is Vancouver's best Italian restaurant, or splash out on contemporary cuisine at the **Hawksworth**, see ③. Catch a band at the **Railway Stage**, see ④, before continuing to **The Diamond** cocktail bar, see ⑤.

Food and drink

① REVOLVER

325 Cambie Street, Gastown; www.revolver coffee.ca; Mon–Fri 7.30am–6pm, Sat 9am–6pm; $$

In a city that's mad for coffee, Revolver reigns supreme for brewing ingenuity. French press, Chemex, aeropress and more, patrons choose their preferred drip method with the help of expert baristas. It's set in two beautiful rooms with exposed brick walls, wood floors, and huge windows perfect for indulging in Gastown people-watching. There's free wi-fi, but seating can be tight.

② CINCIN

1154 Robson Street, between Thurlow and Bute; www.cincin.net; daily 5pm–11pm, bar till midnight; $$$

This long-standing Italian gem has a refined, buzzy setting; try to book an outside table in summer. The food merits the prices (pastas from $24, mains around $34) and their cocktail-creating bartender is one of Canada's finest.

③ HAWKSWORTH RESTAURANT

801 West Georgia Street, at the Rosewood Hotel Georgia; www.hawksworthrestaurant. com; Mon–Fri 6.30am–9.30pm, Sat and Sun 7am–9.30pm; $$$$

Set in Vancouver's most distinguished hotel – the Rosewood Hotel Georgia – Hawksworth serves exquisite Canadian cuisine amid voguish chandeliers with an impressive wine cellar and one of the city's finest cocktail bars. At lunchtime you can soak up the culinary grandeur for a little less.

④ RAILWAY STAGE & BEER CAFÉ

579 Dunsmuir Street, at Seymour, Downtown; tel: 604 564 1430; www.facebook.com/pg/ railwaysbc; Mon–Thu and Sun 11am–2am, Fri & Sat 11am–3am; $$

Housed in the one-time Railway Club (which helped launch artists like k.d. Lang and the Barenaked Ladies), the Railway Stage continues the live music tradition with added DJs and chilled out tap room.

⑤ THE DIAMOND

6 Powell Street #2, Gastown; http://midnight.www.di6mond.com; Mon–Thu 5.30pm–1am, Fri and Sat 5.30pm–2am, Sun 5.30pm–$$$

This charming bar shakes up superlative cocktails for a thirsty crowd of regulars and visiting booze fans. Windows boast bird's-eye views of the area. Step into the second bar to enjoy Happy Hour with retro favourites and a more high-spirited vibe.

HAIDA GWAII

The wild islands of "the Canadian Galapagos" are rich in flora and fauna and Indigenous culture. Learn about the ancient Haida way of life as you explore Graham Island, where thousand-year-old spruce and cedar rainforests meet driftwood-strewn shores.

DISTANCE: 400km (248 miles) return on the ferry and 300km (186 miles) of driving in Haida Gwaii
TIME: 2 days on Haida Gwaii; 16 hour round-trip on the ferry
START/END: Prince Rupert
POINTS TO NOTE: Accommodation is scarce and in demand, so book early or enquire about vacancies at the tourist office. You can bring your own car on the ferry or rent one on Haida Gwaii. Budget (tel: 250 637 5688) in Queen Charlotte can arrange to leave a car for pick-up at the ferry terminal; otherwise, take a six-minute taxi ride from the dock to Queen Charlotte (call licensed 24-hour taxi services Gwaii Taxi and Tours: 250 559 8622; www.gwaiitaxiandtours.ca). Eagle Transit (www.eagletransit.net) runs a weekday public bus service between Queen Charlotte and Masset, with pick-up and drop-off available in most communities.

Arranged in a gentle arc some 150km (93 miles) off the Prince Rupert coast, the two hundred-or-so islands of Haida Gwaii (formerly known as the Queen Charlotte Islands) are something of a cult destination among travellers and environmentalists – for their scenery, wildlife, and almost legendary remoteness from the mainstream.

The two main islands are **Graham Island** (Kiis Gwaay) in the north and **Moresby Island** (T'aawxii X̱aaydag̱a Gwaay.yaay linag̱waay, literally: "south people island half") – and these being the only areas with roads, are the most accessible to independent travellers.

Having escaped the last Ice Age, endemic Haida Gwaii wildlife includes the biggest subspecies of black bear, a subspecies of pine marten, deer mouse, hairy woodpecker, saw-whet owl and Stellar's jay. There are more eagles here than anywhere else in the region, as well as the elusive black-footed albatross – whose wingspan exceeds that of the largest eagle. In the water, there's a good chance of spotting several species of whale, otter, sea lion and other aquatic mammals, schools of fish and a host of colourful marine invertebrates.

Ocean sunset at Haida Gwaii

PRINCE RUPERT

This route starts on mainland at **Prince Rupert ❶**, where BC Ferries (www.bcferries.com) depart near the end of the Yellowhead Highway. Walk-on tickets for foot passengers are rarely a problem at either terminal, but reservations are essential if you're taking a car or want a cabin for any summer crossing. The ferry you want is the MV *Northern Adventure* to Skidegate Landing on Haida Gwaii (www.bcferries.com; early May to late Sept daily; rest of year three weekly).

It lands on Graham Island, the northernmost of the group's two main collections of islands, between the small communities of Queen Charlotte and Skidegate. Under the best weather conditions, there's a crossing time of eight hours (but it can take much longer). For a faster, but more expensive alternative, it is possible to fly from Prince Rupert or Vancouver.

GRAHAM ISLAND

Ferries dock at **Skidegate Landing ❷**, 2km (1.2 miles) to the south of Skidegate on Graham Island's east coast.

The bulk of Graham Island's roads and accommodation is concentrated along its eastern side, between Queen Charlotte in the south and Masset some 108km (67 miles) to the north. These settlements and the villages in between – Skidegate, Tlell and Port Clements – lie along Hwy-16, the principal road, and shelter in the lee of the islands, away from a mountainous and indented rocky west coast that boasts the highest combined seismic, wind and tidal energy of any west-coast North American coastline.

Meanwhile, the east is blessed with beautiful half-moon beaches and a provincial park where you can appreciate the milder climes produced by the Pacific's Japanese Current, a warming stream that contributes to the island's lush canopy of thousand-year-old spruce and cedar rainforests.

Haida Heritage Centre

Before you head off into Haida's tranquility, take some time to look around. At Kaay Llnagaay around 500 metres/yds east of the ferry terminal, take an hour to browse

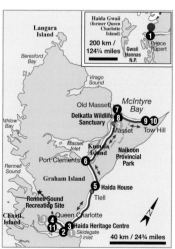

Boardwalk through rainforest, Haida Gwaii

through the accessible aspects of Haida culture at the **Haida Heritage Centre ❸** (Second Beach; www.haidaheritagecentre.com; Tue–Sat 9.30am–5pm).

The centre – a series of longhouses fronted by totem poles – includes a canoe house, a restaurant, a performance space, an art and carving studio and a museum which, among other things, contains a comprehensive collection of the Haida's treasured argillite carvings. In the canoe house you can view the famous Loo Taas ("Wave Eater") canoe, carved by Haida artist Bill Reid. It was made for the Expo '86 world fair in Vancouver and was the first Haida canoe carved since 1909.

Behind the museum there's a lookout deck, from where you might spot grey whales during their migration, between April and June.

The Haida

The Haida are widely considered to have the most highly developed culture and art tradition of BC's First Peoples. Extending from Haida Gwaii to southern Alaska, their lands included major stands of red cedar, the raw material for their huge dugout canoes, their traditional intricate carvings and their homes. The Haida were feared warriors, paddling into rival villages and returning with canoes laden with goods and slaves. Their skill on the open sea made them the "Vikings" of North America.

Grab a bite to eat at the centre's **Green Eggs Market**, see ❶, in front of the ferry terminal, and collect your car, probably from **Queen Charlotte ❹**, a short taxi ride away.

HWY-16

Drive north for around 40 minutes, along the Queen Charlottes Hwy/Yellowhead Hwy W/BC-16 W, aiming for the sleepy, picturesque settlement of **Tlell**. Note that roads off the highway are gravel and many are used by logging trucks.

Take a detour left along Wiggins Road for the **Tlell Artisans' studios and gift shops**, excellent for souvenirs – and you can buy coffee, too.

About 8km (5 miles) beyond the Misty Meadows Campground, turn right onto Beitush Road and you'll reach the eco-adventure lodge, **Haida House ❺**, see page 111. It's spread out over a long stretch of coastline with wind-sculpted dunes. You can easily spend an afternoon here using the kayaks and stand-up paddle boards in the bay. Its remote location makes it ideal for wildlife-spotting – you might even see an endemic black bear.

PORT CLEMENTS

Drive south on Beitush Road and cross the Tlell Bridge, staying on Yellowhead Highway for **Port Clements ❻**, 21km (13 miles) northwest of Tlell. In the past, Port Clements was famous for the Golden Spruce, a 300-year-old bleached albino

Prince Rupert scene

Haida village poles

sitka spruce, sacred to the Haida; in 1997 a protestor chopped it down. A rare genetic mutation allowed the tree's needles to be bleached by sunlight.

A 20-minute trail along the banks of the Yakoun River leads to a viewpoint where you can see where the tree once stood; the trailhead is 6km (3.7 miles) south of town along unsealed Bayview Drive, and 10km (6 miles) further south, look out for the 200-year-old partially carved, abandoned Haida canoe protruding from the bushes.

Pick up Bayview Drive to meet the Yellowhead Highway heading north (20km north of town on the road to Masset, watch for the Pure Lake Provincial Park, a good picnic stop along the lakeshore).

Masset

Masset, 40km (25 miles) north of Port Clements (around a half-hour drive), is the biggest place on the islands, a scattered settlement – it's a former military base – of some 1,000 people, most of whom are employed in the fishing industry. However, it's worth pulling in here (left along Hodges Avenue) for a takeaway snack at **Tow Truck**, see ➋.

OLD MASSETT

The neighbouring village of **Old Massett** ➐ – with an extra "t" – 2km (1.2 miles) to the west along the finger of land, is the administrative centre for the Council of the Haida First Nation and is where some 800 Haida live and work.

Visitors should show respect when visiting totem sites, craft houses and community homes. Many locals are involved in producing crafts for tourists, or organizing wilderness tours, but some are restoring and adding to the dozen or so totems still standing locally.

For more information on where to see carving and on the village in general, call at the **Old Massett Council office** (348 Eagle Avenue; tel: 250 626 3337; Mon–Fri 9am–5pm), where you should also enquire about permission to visit the **Duu Guusd Heritage Site and Conservancy**, established by the Haida to protect villages on the coast to the northwest. Two villages are still active, and the park is used as a base for the Haida Gwaii Rediscovery Centre, which offers courses to children on Haida culture and history.

DELKATLA WILDLIFE SANCTUARY

Many visitors are here for the birdwatching at the **Delkatla Wildlife Sanctuary** ➑, a saltwater marsh north of the village. The sanctuary is home to over 140 bird species, many of which stop over for a brief time while resting and refuelling before commencing their annual spring or fall migrations. Contact Delkatla Bay Birding Tours (tel: 250 626 5015) for guided visits.

TOW HILL

One of the more popular activities in Masset is to walk the trails around **Tow**

Hill ⑨, 26km (16 miles) to the east of Old Massett along Tow Hill Road. The hikes here take in the scenery of Naikoon Provincial Park, an enclave of the northeast part of the island with fine dunes and dwarf-woodland habitats.

Trails

The trails begin by the Hiellen River at the foot of Tow Hill itself. The easiest is the 1km (0.6 mile) **Blow Hole Trail** ⑩, which drops down to striking rock formations and basalt cliffs by the sea. During the right tides and water conditions there is a naturally formed blow hole that shoots water high into the air. From here you can follow another path to the top of Tow Hill (109 metres/357ft) for superb views of deserted sandy beaches stretching into the hazy distance – on a clear day you'll see Alaska, 75km (46 miles) away.

MASSET TO QUEEN CHARLOTTE

Retrace the highway 133km (82 miles) back to the fishing village of **Queen Charlotte** ⑪, a drive of around 1hr 47min. The island's second-largest settlement after Masset, with a smattering of lodges and B&Bs, many visitors use Queen Charlotte as a bouncing off point for tours into the remote parts of Haida Gwaii, for which special arrangements by boat or plane must be made.

If you have the time for one more hike, head to the mountain range the locals call **Sleeping Beauty**, which provides a fine overview of the place from its trails.

For dinner, try the **Ocean Bay Pub and Grill**, see ③. Next morning, drop your car back off or drive to Skidegate, and take the return ferry to Prince Rupert.

Food and drink

① GREEN EGGS MARKET

4920 Hwy 16; Mon–Wed 7.30am–6pm, Thu & Fri 7.30am–9pm, Sat 10am–9pm; $

Revive yourself after the long journey with some grab-and-go refreshments from this healthy snack bar. The light menu includes smoothies, focaccia panini and soups made from scratch, such as vegan coconut lentil curry.

② TOW TRUCK

2083 Collison Avenue, Masset; check www.facebook.com/towtruckmasset for latest opening hours; $$

Locals rave about this gourmet food truck, where the hearty food includes scallop tacos, pork belly burger and poutine.

③ OCEAN VIEW PUB & GRILL

3200 Oceanview Road; http://oceanview restaurant.business.site; Wed & Thu 4pm–11pm, Fri 4pm–2am, Sat noon–2am, Sun noon–9pm; $

As lively a place as you'll find round here, the bar and grill has a respectable selection of brews and a great menu with a seafood focus. There are regular band performances.

Dawson City road sign

DAWSON CITY

Step back into the Klondike gold rush–era with a walk around the centre of the great 1898 stampede. This route takes in Dawson's highlights, from can-can dancers to local curiosities and the cabins of literary legends inspired by the frontier town.

DISTANCE: 3.8km (2.3 miles)
TIME: Half a day. Head out in the afternoon to tag dinner and entertainment onto the route.
START: Cheechakos Bake Shop
END: Diamond Tooth Gertie's Gambling Hall
POINTS TO NOTE: In July and August it's pretty much essential to book accommodation in advance. Prices drop considerably outside the high summer period and many spots close between September and mid-May. Dawson City's airport is 19km (12 miles) southeast of the town on the Klondike Highway. You can arrive by car along this road (see Route 13); it takes around six hours from Whitehorse, or from Alaska via the Top of the World Highway (open May–Sept).

Few episodes in Canadian history have captured the imagination like the Klondike gold rush, and few places have remained as evocative of their past as Dawson City, the stampede's tumultuous capital where fortunes were won and lost.

For a couple of months in 1898 this former patch of moose pasture became one of the wealthiest and most famous places on earth. There was nothing quite like the delirium of the Klondike gold rush. Over 100,000 people are estimated to have left home for the region, the largest single one-year mass movement of people that century. About 30,000 made it, but only 4,000 found any gold. A couple of dozen of these made – and lost – huge fortunes.

The town that's left, with a permanent population of just 1,500, is a place to glimpse the past, with its fascinating atmosphere of faded grandeur. Visitors spend a day or two here, exploring the boardwalks, dirt streets and false-fronted wooden houses, particularly those in the street grid behind Front Street, which runs parallel to the Yukon River.

Parks Canada is restoring designated National Historic Sites, but in a spot where permafrost buckles buildings, snow falls in late September and temperatures touch -60°C (-76F) during winters, there's little real chance of Dawson losing the gritty, weather-worn feel of a true frontier town.

SS Keno

FRONT STREET

Begin the route on **Front Street ❶**, a long row of colourful frontier-style buildings lining a wide unpaved road. At **Cheechakos Bakeshop**, see ❶, try a pecan-topped sticky bun, then walk a minute north (right from the bakery).

Browse until your heart's content at **Maximilian's Gold Rush Emporium** (www.maximilians.ca; summer daily 9am–8pm, winter Mon–Sat 10am–6pm, Sun noon–5pm). This independent store is most known for its paperbacks on local history and the latest fiction; it's also the place to pick up Yukon-themed gifts such as maple products and tees.

Vintage riverboats

Continue north to the charming **SS Keno** riverboat ❷, berthed in a dry dock on the waterfront. A vintage beauty from 1922, it ran up and down the Stewart River carrying ore from the mines around Mayo. Guided summer tours feature a photo exhibit, "Dawson City in the 1950s."

Not all boats were as lucky as the Keno; the improvements to transportation links made many riverboats redundant and some were beached downstream. If you have the time, cross the river on the free ferry, walk through the campground and ten more minutes along the waterfront and you'll reach a **Paddlewheel Graveyard**, strewn dramatically with the ruins of seven boats.

Otherwise, keep walking up Front Street, to the striking-looking **Dänojà**

Zho Cultural Centre ❸ (www.trondek heritage.com; June–Sept Mon–Sat 10am–6pm; by appointment rest of year), or "Long Time Ago House." Exhibits, guides, videos and live demonstrations explore both the traditional and present-

Dawson City aerial view　　　　　*Dawson City street*

day culture of the Tr'ondëk Hwëch'in, the region's original inhabitants.

A little further, set slightly back from the road, is the **Firefighter Museum ④** (www.dawsonfirefightermuseum.com; May–Sept 11am–5pm; by appointment rest of year; donation). Established in 1898 during the Gold Rush era, tours of vintage fire engines, water pumps and other artifacts are available. In a town built almost entirely of wood, these were once vital to Dawson's survival.

Backtrack slightly, then turn left down Duke Street at the Yukon Sawmill Co. You can now take any street parallel to Front Street to the centre of town; the first one you come to, a backstreet of eclectic porches, provides an insight into residential Dawson life.

Galleries

After around seven minutes, you'll hit Princess Street, and turning left, look out for lime-green **Klondike Institute of Art and Culture ⑤**. This contemporary art gallery and residence programme brings over 18 artists to town each year.

Walking left as you exit, the next building along is **Harrington's Store**, where a "Dawson As They Saw It" exhibition of photos from the mining era is shown (June–Sept daily 9am–4.30pm; free).

SOUTH OF TOWN

Cross the road and walk down Third Avenue beside the Red Feather Saloon. If you like, order coffee from **BonTon & Company**, see ②, when it comes up on your right. The next part of the route takes you into a quieter, sparer part of town, and reveals the literary characters who were attracted to Dawson City.

Writers' cabins

Walk for nine minutes (700 metres/ 2,296ft), turning left at Church Street and then right down Eighth Avenue to the **Robert Service Cabin ⑥** (Eighth Avenue and Hanson Avenue; tours July–Sept; charge, but free 2–3pm). Robert Service earned his place in the pantheon of Canadian literature with verses like *The Shooting of Dan McGrew* and *The Cremation of Sam McGee* evoking the myth of the North. He retired a rich man on the proceeds of his writing.

His **cabin**, which is a very accurate restoration, gives an idea of how most people must have lived once Dawson was reasonably established. During the summer people come here to pay homage and listen to a Parks Canada staffer read one or two of the writer's poems.

Opposite is the **Berton House Writers' Retreat**. It was built in 1901 and was the childhood home of another famous Canadian writer, Pierre Berton, whose bestseller *Klondike – The Last Great Gold Rush 1896–1899* offers a superb insight into this time in Canadian history. The house now acts as a private retreat for Canadian writers.

Continue on the same street for another minute to **Jack London's Cabin ⑦** (corner of Eighth Avenue and Firth

Jack London's Cabin

Street; mid-May to mid-Sept daily) is a somewhat unpersuasive piece of reconstruction (logs from the original were separated and half of them used to build a cabin in Jack London Square in Oakland, California). However, alongside the hut there's a great little museum of pictures and memorabilia, where docents tell stories of London's life and work during the summer (noon and 3pm).

Food and drink

① CHEECHAKOS BAKESHOP
902 Front Street; tel: 867 993 5303; May–Sept Mon–Fri 7am–5.30pm, Sat and Sun 9am–4pm; $
A cosy café offering home-baked breads, pastries, cakes and muffins along with breakfast and lunch sandwiches.

② BONTON & COMPANY
878 Third Avenue; tel: 867 993 4194; Tue–Wed 9am–5.30pm, Thu–Fri, 9am–10pm, Sat 11am–10pm; $$
Coffee shop by day, small plates restaurant by night (reservations essential), BonTon has a neighbourhood deli feel and a passion for food sustainability.

③ DRUNKEN GOAT TAVERNA
950 Second Avenue; tel: 867 993 5868; daily noon–10pm year-round; $$
One of the most popular restaurants in town, it specializes in Greek food, served in hearty portions by a very friendly staff.

Food and entertainment

Shoot north up Seventh Avenue and back into the centre. At this point you can head for dinner at the **Drunken Goat Taverna**, see ③, if it's after 5pm.

Or, turn left onto Queen Street if you want to get your entertainment started, at **Diamond Tooth Gertie's Gambling Hall ⑧** (www.diamondtoothgerties.ca; Fourth Avenue and Queen Street; mid-May to mid-Sept daily 7pm–2am, Fri–Sun from 2pm; off-season Fri and Sat only).

Canada's oldest legal gambling hall, it was the first legal casino in Canada when it opened in 1971 with a name inspired by one of the town's more notorious characters. It's still operating, and is now also the world's northernmost casino. Three times a night, a singer and can-can girls grace the stage for some over-the-top pantie-revealing, tap-dancing and (mostly tame) titillating audience interaction. You need to be over 19 to gamble and all proceeds from here and several other town sights go to the maintenance of the visitor attractions and to the community of Dawson.

If you are staying for longer, make a point of seeing the two creeks where it all started and where most of the gold was mined – Bonanza and Eldorado, both over 20km (12 miles) from Dawson City along rough roads to the southeast. Today, gold mining continues at a hectic pace as more claims are being staked and deposits discovered – most of these claims are still owned and definitely out of bounds to amateurs.

Klondike Highway

KLONDIKE HIGHWAY

Make a dramatic entrance to Dawson City (Route 12) on the Klondike Highway from Whitehorse, the Yukon's capital. Especially beautiful in fall, this wonderful, lonely road often feels like wilderness, but has all the conveniences you need along the way.

DISTANCE: 536km (333 miles)

TIME: 2 days, 3 if you add a tour in Whitehorse

START: Whitehorse

END: Dawson City

POINTS TO NOTE: You can get a bus from Skagway to Whitehorse and then another from Whitehorse to Dawson City. Husky Bus (www.klondike experience.com) operates a scheduled service from Whitehorse visitor centre (2nd Avenue and Lambert Street) to Dawson City (2 or 3 weekly; 7hr).

enough overproof rum to keep the drivers sufficiently lubricated).

Today, the drive takes little more than six hours, but it's all the more enjoyable for stretching that out over a couple of days, including time in Whitehorse, frequent stops, and a detour along the Silver Trail to explore the historic silver-mining town of Mayo.

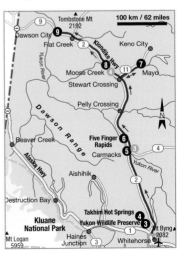

The Klondike Highway (536km/333 miles in total) is divided into two parts, the South Klondike from Skagway (in Alaska) and the North Klondike – this route – from Whitehorse to Dawson City.

The road loosely follows the original winter overland route to the Yukon's goldfields, first used in 1902. Then, it took five days to complete the chilly journey in horse-drawn stages, with the trip costing an extortionate $125 per person (passengers were also expected to carry

Red Fox

WHITEHORSE

Whitehorse 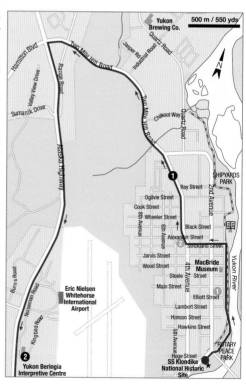 is the likeable capital of the Yukon and home to more than 25,000 of the region's 35,000 inhabitants. Though now graced only with a handful of pioneer buildings, the place still retains the dour integrity and appealing energy of a frontier town, and at night the baying of timber wolves and coyotes are a reminder of the wilderness immediately beyond the city limits.

If you have a day to spare, complete the Klondike experience with a ten-hour round trip to Skagway – Alaska's designated Klondike Gold Rush National Historical Park. A coach takes you to Fraser, BC, where the tour connects with the dramatic narrow-gauge White Pass & Yukon Route Railway, before allowing you two hours to explore Skagway. Booking is required (www.wpyr.com) and check on any border restrictions in advance. Leave your vehicle in Whitehorse or begin your rental the following day.

If you're drinking or day-tripping, you'll need to spend the night in town. Get a good meal at

Dirty Northern Public House, see ❶, before bunking down.

SS Klondike

Even if you're not spending the night in Whitehorse, before you set off, there are a couple of key sights for which you should make time. **SS Klondike** (2nd Avenue at 300 Main Street; mid-May to

SS Klondike   *MacBride Museum*

Aug daily 9.30am–5pm; free self-guided tours or paid guided tours, check with the visitors' centre).

Launched in 1937, it plied the river until 1950. One of only two surviving paddle steamers in the Yukon, it's rather sadly beached at the western end of 2nd Avenue, although it has been beautifully restored to the glory of its 1930s heyday. The other remaining paddle wheeler, the SS *Keno*, rests in Dawson City.

Housed in a log cabin, the **MacBride Museum** (Front Street and Wood Street; www.macbridemuseum.com; tel: 867 667 2709; May–Aug daily 9.30am–7.30pm; Sept–May Tue–Sat 10am–4pm or by appointment) is packed with taxidermized animals (including an albino moose), an old WP&YR engine, pioneer and gold-rush memorabilia, as well as hundreds of marvellous archive photos and a display on the Asiatic peoples who crossed the Bering Straits to inhabit the Americas. For an extra $5 you can try your luck at panning for gold (summer only).

SETTING OFF ON THE KLONDIKE

If you don't have a car with you, in the morning pick up a rental from **Budget** (4178 4th Avenue; www.budget.ca). Visit the **Alpine Bakery**, see ❷, for provisions as you exit the city. From 4th Avenue, drive north on Two Mile Hill Road and you'll see the Klondike Highway signed.

However, at this point it's worth going slightly out of your way to visit the dynamic **Yukon Beringia Interpretive Centre** ❷

(www.beringia.com) and driving south instead of north on the Klondike Highway. Beringia was the vast subcontinent that existed 24,000 years ago when the Yukon and Alaska were joined by a land bridge across the Bering Sea to Arctic Russia. The centre's interactive exhibits, films and displays explore the Indigenous history of the time. The flora, fauna and geology of that period are also covered and displays include the remains of a 12,000-year-old mammoth.

From there, drive for about 20 minutes north and take the left for Takhini Hot Springs Road at the gas station, which brings you to the **Yukon Wildlife Preserve** ❸ www.yukonwildlife.ca; (mid-May to mid-Oct daily 9.30am–6pm; mid-Oct to mid-May usually Fri–Sun only, call ahead to confirm hours; self-guided walk or guided bus tour) 8km (5 miles) later. The

Flying visit

When it comes to getting around the Yukon, one option worth considering is the Yukon Advantage Traveller Air Pass, offered by Air North (www.flyairnorth. com), which allows you 10 segments to fly to or from seven destinations with Whitehorse as a hub (so all flights must begin or pass through that city). The pass covers up to two people, and all segments must be flown within one year. It's also pretty flexible, with reservations possible up to one hour before flight and low change/cancel fees.

Northern lights on display

11 types of mammal that graze the large expanses here are largely of the hoofed variety, such as heavily-antlered caribou or impressive moose that slowly amble from the rear of their swampy enclosure to appear huge nearer your path, or endlessly entertaining mountain goats.

Two kilometres (1.2 miles) further down the road comes the **Takhini Hot Springs** ❹ (www.takhinihotsprings.com; daily noon–10pm, extended hours in summer), where the water in the large pool is a toasty 36°C (96.8°F). You can camp or dock your RV here ($20–42) or park yourself in the hostel ($30, $100 for a private room) and if you don't want to pay for the privilege of a hot soak, use the public pool at the outflow point in the stream below, built by the locals.

CARMACKS

Carmacks ❺ is the first settlement of any note you'll hit. It has two gas stations and a visitor centre, but its prime location at a wide hairpin bend of the Yukon River makes it a good activity base. Push on a little further, crossing the river, and **Coal Mine Campground & Canteen**, see page 111, will be on your right. It's at the junction of the Robert Campbell Hwy, later a scenic gravel road winding 590km (366 miles) east to Watson Lake. The campground is a relaxing place to take in the view of the Yukon River while munching on a burger or enjoying an ice cream cone, see ❸. You can choose between tent sites, RV sites and cabins

and there's bike rentals, showers, laundry and free wi-fi.

Just after the bridge leaving Carmacks, the **Tagé Cho Hudän Interpretive Centre** (tel: 867 863 5831; summer daily 9am–6pm or by appointment) has exhibits revealing something of the traditional lifestyle of the Northern Tutchone people.

About 25km (15.5km) north of Carmacks, stop off at the lookout for the formidable **Five Finger Rapids** ❻, to your left. Formed by five huge pillars that divide the Yukon River into narrow channels, many a stampeder lost his belongings here – or worse, his life. A steep 1km (0.6 mile) trail leads down from the lookout to the water's edge.

STEWART CROSSING

A further 153km (95 miles) north, the village of **Stewart Crossing** sits at the junction of the **Silver Trail**, a highway that strikes off northeast for three historic silver-mining towns that sprang up following the discovery of silver on Keno Hill in 1919. There's a visitor kiosk (summer) just after the turn-off for the Silver Trail.

If you've got time for a detour, leave the highway by turning right up the winding 56km (34.7 miles) drive to **Mayo** ❼, through moose habitat.

STEWART CROSSING TO DAWSON CITY

The route's scenery is at its best after Stewart Crossing, for the last stretch of

Mammoth outside Yukon Beringia Interpretive Centre

the Klondike Highway, with wide views of sweeping valleys, rounded mountains and drunken forests (the spruce trees here all lean to one side thanks to the underlying permafrost which stunts growth). At the 554km (334-mile) mark, a bright red hand-painted sign welcomes you to **Moose Creek** ⑧, Yukon's smallest town, home to "two great guys and gals and three friendly dogs", and a lovely little place to stop for a bite to eat, see ④, or to spend the night. It's also the last place on the highway to fuel up before Dawson.

Some 40km (25 miles) before Dawson City is the turn-off for the **Dempster Highway**. The 741km (460 miles) of this road between Dawson City and Inuvik (12–15hr) in the Northwest Territories is the only road in Canada to cross the Arctic Circle.

Just before Dawson City, the road wanders through tree-covered hills and then picks up a small, ice-clear river – the **Klondike**. The first small spoil heaps start to appear on the hills to the south, and then suddenly the entire valley bottom turns into a devastated landscape of vast boulders and abandoned dredge tailings. This continues for several kilometres until the Klondike flows into the much broader **Yukon River**, and **Dawson City** ⑨ comes suddenly into view.

Food and drink

① DIRTY NORTHERN PUBLIC HOUSE

103 Main Street; tel: 867 663 3305; www.dirtynorthernyukon.com; daily 11.30am–2pm; $$

A hip crowd hangs at the Dirty Northern, lured in with the promise of 10 beers on tap, a handful of in-house cocktails, live music (some nights) and tweaked pub food. Try the bacon vanilla ice cream sandwich.

② ALPINE BAKERY

411 Alexander Street; tel: 867 668 6871; www.alpinebakery.ca; Mon–Fri 8am–6pm, Sat 8am–4pm; $$

The bread, pizza slices, soups, cakes and freshly squeezed juices are all made from organic ingredients at this popular bakery.

③ COAL MINE CAMPGROUND & CANTEEN

1 Mile North of Carmacks; tel: 867 863-6363; www.coalminecampground.com; $

There's something about the mighty scene of the winding forest-backed river and fresh Yukon air that makes the bacon double cheeseburger and milkshakes at this campsite's café taste extra good.

④ MOOSE CREEK LODGE

561 North Klondike Hwy, Mayo; tel: 867-996-2550, www.moosecreek-lodge.com; $$

Thanks to their on-site greenhouse, Moose Creek Lodge offers fresh veg and salads (all organically grown) year-round as part of their breakfasts, lunches and dinners. A couple of pastries-to-go certainly perk up the rest of the journey, too.

YELLOWKNIFE, NORTHWEST TERRITORIES

As the capital of the unimaginably vast Northwest Territories, Yellowknife sits at the edge of a wonderous northern frontier – but this city's unique character, encapsulated by March's Snowking Festival, makes it more than just a springboard for tours.

DISTANCE: 10km (6 miles) without Tincan hike
TIME: Two days to allow for tours
START/END: McDonald Drive
POINTS TO NOTE: Practice extreme caution when walking on ice. Stick to the well-trodden areas, even when the ice looks solid, unless accompanied by a guide. You do not need a car for this route. Frontier Coachlines (www.frontiercoachlinesnwtltd.ca) runs three buses weekly to Yellowknife from Hay River via Fort Smith. Yellowknife's airport is 5km (3 miles) west of the city on Hwy-3; a taxi from there costs around $20. Call City Cab (tel: 867 873 4444) or Diamond (tel: 867 873 6666).

The Northwest Territories occupies a third of Canada's landmass – about the size of India – but contains only 41,000 people, almost half of whom live in or around Yellowknife.

Surrounded by an endless expanse of lakes, forests and great wilderness, Yellowknife is named after the copper knives of the First Nations Slavey people. Today, this city draws adventure seekers who come to experience it's legendary hospitality, its Northern Lights and an array of cultural events. Despite its large-city size, Yellowknife has managed to keep its frontier-town atmosphere.

Clothing rental

First thing's first: if you're here for the Snowking Festival in March, the average temperature is around -19°C (-2.2°F), so if you don't already have the right kit, you may want to buy some to keep you toasty for your trip. **Weaver and Devore ❶** provides all the cold-weather clothing you'll need, including toques, mitts and boots, plus groceries and other outdoor gear. Alternatively, many tour operators allow clients to borrow clothing as part of the package.

Accommodation

Hotel prices in this city are high, so it's worth looking up one of the dozen or so **B&Bs** if you're on a budget. One of the best is the **Bayside B&B**, see page 111. Located in the heart of Old Town

Aurora village

and on the shore of Great Slave Lake, there's also an all-day café downstairs (**Dancing Moose**, see ①) with a deck. Floatplane mooring facilities are available if you're flash enough to fly in.

Old Town

Visitors are steered carefully up the main street, Franklin Avenue (50th Avenue), from the Old Town. It's a shakedown of pitted and buckled roads (the result of permafrost) and a few quaintly battered cabins on the aptly named Ragged Ass Road and Willow Road. These are more or less the only remnants of the old times, but there is an exciting feeling of being on the edge of nowhere – which, of course, you are. A great place to get coffee around here is the **Wildcat Café**, see ②.

Also in this end of town is the **Old Town Glassworks** ②, which hosts glass etching workshops that let you get creative and leave with a unique piece of your own hand-crafted memorabilia from Yellowknife (3510 Mcdonald Drive; Tue–Fri and Sat, 2 hours). Its mission is to repurpose used glass bottles and other wasted glass into beautiful new glassware; everyone receives one piece of the glassworks' recycled products from the workshop.

SNOWKING FESTIVAL

Yellowknife springs to life during its many annual festivals, the most intriguing of which is **Snowking Festival** ③. Attractions during the month-long party in March include a Snow Castle, snowcarv-

ing competition, fireworks, art exhibits, a film festival and plenty of music and food (www.snowking.ca; usually Tues–Sun noon–5pm).

Located on the frozen expanse of **Great Slave Lake** on Yellowknife Bay, beside Old Town's Woodyard neighbourhood, as soon as the castle's constructed it becomes a hub of activity. In this eccentric tradition, which features a slide made of ice, the festival's founder is referred to as "Snowking" and his court include the likes of Joe Snow Baron Von Blizzard.

Taxis are available to and from the castle. If you're walking, turn right on Hamilton Drive, walk straight for two blocks until you see the entrance to the Woodyard shack. Keep on the path through the trees, and you will come out directly behind the castle.

Ice fishing

Another activity to do on Great Slave Lake (the deepest lake in North America at 614 meters/2,015ft) is a half-day ice fishing tour with Arctic Tours Canada (www.arctictourscanada.ca; 3 hours; pick-up at 11am from selected hotels). Cast your line into an 8-inch drilled hole on the frozen lake, either inside or outside a heated fishing tent, stocked with hot drinks. A fish lunch is also part of the deal.

Food and drink

Yellowknife is increasingly becoming known for its fantastic range of restaurants that serve up everything from traditional pub fare to unique northern cuisine

House boats in Yellowknife Bay

such as caribou, musk ox and arctic char. Most of the hotels have good dining rooms and much of the nightlife revolves around their lounges. The **Bullocks Bistro**, see ③, is the best place in town to try locally sourced cuisine. Near to the Snow Castle, the **NWT Brewing Company**, see ④, continues the theme of local produce.

Prince of Wales Northern Heritage Centre

On your second day, walk to downtown along Franklin Ave, turning right at 49 Street and onto the path through the trees you'll see on your right. Your destination is the **Prince of Wales Northern Heritage Centre ❹** (4750 48 Street; www.pwnhc. ca; daily 10.30am–5.30pm, Thu until 9pm; free), on the shore of Frame Lake.

As Yellowknife's key attraction, the centre showcases the culture, heritage and history of the Northwest Territories. The permanent Tundra and Taiga galleries highlight the landscapes and cultures from above and below the treeline respectively, and other exhibits feature topics such as ice age mammals, the Yellowknives Dene First Nation, Indigenous Special Constables and the RCMP. The community exhibit and contemporary art spaces showcase different works every six months and the centre also includes a café and an interactive children's area.

YELLOWKNIFE HIKES

The museum is ideally located for nearby trails around **Frame Lake ❺**. Bear west,

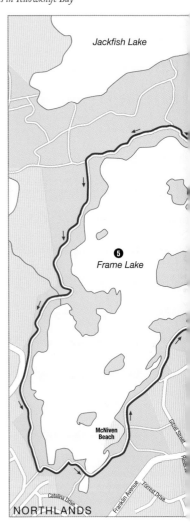

Jackfish Lake

Frame Lake

McNiven Beach

Catalina Drive

NORTHLANDS

Franklin Avenue

Forrest Drive

Old Airport Road

Prince of Wales Northern HC

Snowking Festival

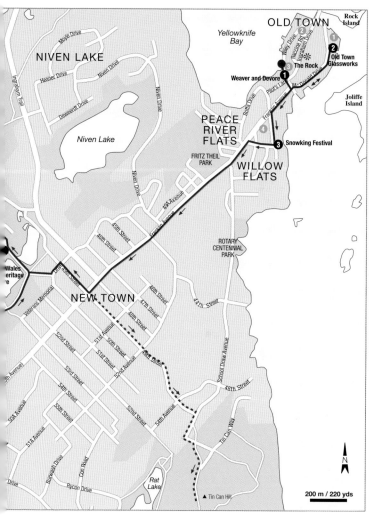

away from downtown Yellowknife, and after around 17 minutes you'll reach the trail. It's a 5.3km (3.3-mile) loop, with opportunities to spot red fox and occasionally coyotes.

AURORA VILLAGE

March is one of the best times to see the Northern Lights – and the Northwest Territories one of the world's best places to see them.

Offering pick-ups from several hotels in Yellowknife, Aurora Village operates a bus that drives you 25 minutes to a Northern Lights viewing location, its "village" of 21 teepees serving as a magical place to see one of the most phenomenal displays on Earth. Heated outdoor viewing seats swivel 360 degrees, so you can catch every angle of the dancing lights as they swirl.

Some packages include dinner (Thu–Sat 5–11pm, Sun 4–9pm).

Food and drink

1 WILDCAT CAFÉ
3904 Wiley Road; www.facebook.com/wildcatyellowknife; June–Sept Mon–Fri 11.30am–10pm, Sat and Sun 10.30am–9pm; $$$

An atmospheric and endlessly busy little café in a log cabin, this is Yellowknife's oldest restaurant, operating since 1937. This Canadian landmark has served everyone from royalty to prime ministers and international celebrities. Expect to share a table while you enjoy a taste of the region ranging from grilled arctic char to bison stew or a veggie burger.

2 DANCING MOOSE CAFÉ
3505 McDonald Drive; tel: 867 669 8844; Mon–Sat 8am–3pm; $$

Perhaps the best place in town for breakfast, this charming café, with a panoramic view, offers a choice of waffles, omelettes and eggs Benedict, as well as lunch items

including soups, sandwiches and home-cooked comfort foods.

3 BULLOCKS BISTRO
3534 Weaver Drive tel: 867 873 3474; Tue–Sat noon–9pm, Sun and Mon 4–9pm; $$$

Fish and chips meets fine dining in this informal, yet fairly high-end restaurant. You'll find simply prepared local whitefish, cod, pike and trout on the menu, along with some delicious chowders and mouth-watering musk-ox stew. Reservations recommended.

4 NWT BREWING COMPANY
3905 Franklin Avenue; Tue–Thu 4–11pm, Fri 11.30am–midnight, Sat noon–midnight, Sun 10am–3pm; http://nwtbrewingco.com; $$$

Canadian-grown grains and the purest water in the world create the unique beers at NWT — a family-run, small batch brewery, where all the brewing is done off-grid. It's attached to its own brewpub, The Woodyard Brewhouse & Eatery.

Mount Thor

NUNAVUT

Canada's largest and newest territory, Nunavut, is the most sparsely populated habitable place on Earth. But for those willing to brave the inhospitable Arctic Circle, the payoff is immense: diverse wildlife, rich native culture and sublime scenery that most people will never see.

DISTANCE: Vast. But Canadian North makes the round-trip daily to Inukpak from Montréal and Ottawa (3.5 hours). Flights also run from Edmonton and Yellowknife.

TIME: Anything from a half-day excursion to expedition trips

POINTS TO NOTE: Hotel prices are invariably per person, not per room, but often include meals. Don't be surprised if you are required to share a room with a stranger – this is the North and hotel space is at a premium.

Home to only 38,000 people, Nunavut covers almost 2 million square km (772,204 sq miles) – a fifth of Canada's land surface and an area five times the size of California. A vast terrain of barren ground, plateaus, ancient fjords and mountains, this landscape is a hauntingly beautiful retreat.

Exploring Nunavut is hugely rewarding but far from easy. As there are virtually no roads, travel by air, snowmobile or dogsled are the only options, and while almost every little community has a serviceable hotel/restaurant, room and food prices are shockingly high.

Although isolated and expensive, the delights of Nunavut's great outdoors are drawing an increasing number of visitors. Outfitters arrange all sorts of packages from building igloos to polar-bear watching, dogsledding, and encounters with narwhals – one-tusked whales at one time believed to be cousins to the mythical unicorn.

BAFFIN ISLAND

The main tourist destination in Nunavut is Baffin Island, the fifth-largest island in the world, half a million square kilometres of Arctic vastness. Its main attraction is Auyuittuq National Park on the Cumberland Peninsula, one of Canada's northernmost accessible national parks. With a treeless landscape, mountains towering over 1,500 metres (4,921ft), icy glacial streams and 24-hour daylight from May to July, hiking in the park offers one of the country's most majestic experiences. Yet with temperatures hitting a

Walrus

mere 10°C (50°F) from June to August, it can be a harsh environment that will appeal only to the intrepid; expensive though they are, package tours are definitely recommended if this is your first venture into such a remote place. Bring all necessary gear with you, as supplies are limited here.

IQALUIT

Located on the southeast of Baffin Island, Nunavut's capital Iqaluit – where the majority of commercial flights land – serves as a gateway to the wilderness.

The growing settlement of 8,000, predominantly Inuit inhabitants, has the most to see in terms of culture and in-town attractions of any built-up area in Nunavut. While the real draws are undoubtedly in the surrounding area, they are highly expensive to reach, so flying to Iqaluit is a way to experience the Arctic without signing up for a package tour.

You'd also have access to the multiple short excursions that take place in and around the town. Igloo-building, snow-sailing and hiking on the tundra are just a few activities available during a stay in Iqaluit, provided by the local com-

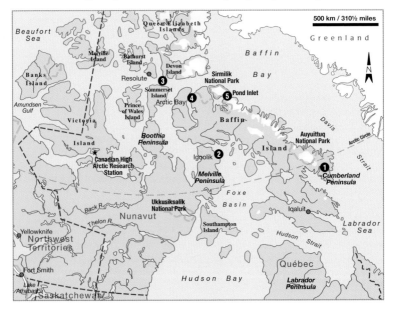

Akshayuk Pass   *Polar bear on Baffin Island*

pany Inukpak Outfitting (www.inukpak outfitting.ca).

EXPEDITIONS

An array of multi-day tours and expeditions are available departing from Iqaluit. Arctic Kingdom (www.arctickingdom.com) and Black Feather (www.blackfeather.com) offer multi-day trips, in addition to Inukpak Outfitting. The options below give you a flavour of what is possible – all pleasures for which you'd pay a pretty price – but may serve as inspiration for budding Nunavut travellers.

Cumberland Peninsula:
Akshayuk Pass to Mount Thor
One way to get up-close to the Nunavut landscape is on a multi-day trek on the **Cumberland Peninsula ❶**, setting up camp each night as you go. You'll also be part of the select group who can say they have crossed the Arctic Circle on foot.

Walrus and bowhead whale watching in Igloolik
Focusing on two of the far north's most awesome animals, the search takes you to Igloolik ❷, on an island at the western edge of the Foxe Basin, adjacent to Baffin. Travelling with Inuit through the environment of water and ice, it is also the time to experience the 24-hour warm Arctic light.

Arctic Express Canada: The Heart of the Northwest Passage
The fabled **Northwest Passage ❸** fasci-

nated legendary explorers of long ago, as they searched for the great sea route at the top of the world. Marine vessel technology means unprecedented access to the High Arctic's icy inlets, channels and bays – previously some of the hardest-to-reach places on the planet. Board a charter flight to Resolute, Nuvanut and then transfer via Zodiac or helicopter to the ship, *Ultramarine*. On board, you'll learn about the scientific, cultural and environmental aspects of the route from experts and the local communities. Wildlife sightings are almost guaranteed.

Arctic in bloom
On Baffin Island, the remote hamlet **Arctic Bay ❹** is a small, welcoming community where you can get to know the traditions, culture and stories of the Inuit peoples who have lived on this land for over 5,000 years. A highlight is the hike up the flat-topped King George Mountain, for a breathtaking view of Arctic Bay and Victor Bay and a vantage point to spot wildlife.

Baffin Island Floe Edge:
Narwhals and Polar Bears
Travel to **Pond Inlet ❺** and camp at the floe edge of northern Baffin Island in the company of naturalist guides, for a wildlife-focused wilderness experience. Travelling in *komatiks* (sleds) for the most part, there are optional hikes on the tundra as well. This is one of the world's best chances to spot a unicorn-tusked narwhal.

DIRECTORY

Hand-picked hotels and restaurants to suit all budgets and tastes, organised by area, plus select nightlife listings and an overview of the best books and films to give you a flavour of the country.

Fogo Island Inn's striking location

ACCOMMODATION

Part of the magic of travelling in Canada is discovering its characterful inns, family-owned B&Bs, boutique holiday homes and wilderness retreats set in astonishing scenery. In a single trip, you could easily experience them all.

Luxury hotels are clustered in the cities and iconic tourist areas, such as the Rockies, which has sprouted a plethora of high-end resorts. Plenty of city hotels take in a birdseye view from flash skyscrapers, but there's also a premium on hotels with historic character, with old landmark buildings frequently reincarnating as five-star abodes.

Away from these hotspots, hotel prices generally drop (other than at Newfoundland's Fogo Island Inn, Canada's most expensive hotel). When you're looking for a mid-priced hotel – around the $150 mark – there are plenty of unique, independently run places, as well as comfortable chain hotels, where breakfast is usually included.

The cheapest rooms are often hangovers from the days when liquor laws made it difficult to run a bar without an adjoining restaurant or hotel. Found in most medium- and small-sized towns, they may be basic but have the advantage of being extremely central. A cheap bed in a hostel dorm, too, is available in many towns.

Then, there are the campgrounds: few countries offer as much scope for camping as Canada. Generally, reservations can only be made with ease at private campgrounds, not – crucially – at national park or provincial park campgrounds (check www.reservation.pc.gc.ca for details).

If you're heading into remote parts of the country, check the availability of accommodation before setting off. Places that look large on the map often have few facilities so it's best to try to book a room before you arrive. Local tourist information offices will invariably help out with accommodation if you get stuck: most offer free advice and will book a place free of charge.

Newfoundland: Gros Morne

Bonne Bay Inn

145 Main Road, Woody Point; tel: 709 453 2223; www.woodypointmagic.com; $$
The view across Bonne Bay is the highlight of this inn, located on the southern shore. Inside it's modern, with comfy beds in the 10 rooms, a lobby sitting area (great for afternoon tea) and the Elements pub on site.

> Price guide for a double room with bathroom for one night:
> $$$$ = over $300
> $$$ = $230–300
> $$ = $130–230
> $ = below $130

A room with a view at Fogo Island Inn

Neddies Harbour Inn

7 Beach Road, Norris Point; tel: 709 458 3089; www.theinn.ca; $$

The sun deck and bar look across the water at Neddies, on the northern side of the bay. Stylish rooms are decked out with local beechwood in a contemporary design, reflecting the sensibilities of the Swiss owners.

Newfoundland: Twillingate

Hillside B&B

14 Blanford's Lane; tel: 709 884 1666; www.bbcanada.com/nfhillside; $

One of the best places to stay in Twillingate, Hillside is an attractive, well-kept B&B in an 1870s clapboard house overlooking the harbour; it has three en-suite rooms, each decorated in simple modern style, and a cottage with a veranda.

Newfoundland: Fogo

Fogo Island Inn

210 Main Road (Hwy-334), Joe Batt's Arm; tel: 709 658 3444; www.fogoislandinn.ca; $$$$

Dominating the horizon is this stilt-raised, purpose-built five-star hotel featuring floor-to-ceiling windows, ocean views and luxurious contemporary rooms. It's a spectacular but exclusive experience, with rooms priced accordingly. Full-board only. Non-guests can take a short tour.

Nova Scotia

Duncreigan Country Inn

11411 Nova Scotia Trunk 19, Mabou; tel: 902 945 2207; $$

It might have been built in the 1990s, but this characterful Mabou inn evokes a far earlier feel with its chintz details and antiques. Some of the eight rooms have whirlpool baths and although there's no restaurant, a buffet breakfast is included.

Ocean View Motel & Chalets

15569 Main Street (Cabot Trail), Chéticamp; tel: 902 224 2313; www.oceanviewchalets. com; $$

Chéticamp has around 20 motels and B&Bs and this is one of the best: 12 well-maintained, spacious chalets and six motel rooms are right on the waterfront, with views of Chéticamp Island (accessed by road).

New Brunswick

Cleveland Place B&B

8580 Main Street (Hwy-114), Alma; tel: 506 887 221; www.bbcanada.com/137.html; $$

Alma's beautiful clapboard B&B dates back to 1927 and is hosted by gourmet chefs. The warm hospitality and food are the highlights, but the airy, period rooms are very comfy and there's a bookstore at the back.

Hilton Saint John Hotel

1 Market Square, Saint John; tel: 506 693 8484; www.3.hilton.com; $$

Most rooms have waterfront views at this plush, modern tower block right beside Market Slip. Location and amenities (it has an indoor pool) are top-class, though you'll pay extra for parking ($20/day) and wi-fi ($6.95/day, free in public areas).

Hilton Saint John

Prince Edward Island

Shaw's Hotel & Cottages

99 Apple Tree Road, Brackley Beach; tel: 902 672 2022; www.shawshotel.ca; $$

The pick of PEI's resort and cottage complexes, Shaw's has charmingly rustic rooms and year-round chalets occupying extensive grounds, about 10 minutes' walk from the beach. It also offers canoe, kayak and bike rental for guests and non-guests.

Shipwright Inn

51 Fitzroy Street, Charlottetown; tel: 902 368 1905; www.shipwrightinn.com; $$

Crammed with antiques, this rambling 1865 timber mansion (with a more recent extension) has nine individually decorated guest rooms managed by a couple of affable British expats. Thoughtful additions (like popcorn and muffins), and superlative breakfasts, add to the appeal.

Montréal

Auberge Bonaparte

447 rue St-François-Xavier tel: 514 844 1448; www.bonaparte.com; $$$

Sleep amid history at this handsome inn shaded by smart burgundy awnings, steps from the Basilique Notre-Dame. The hotel was built in 1886 and rooms are decked out with wrought-iron headboards, hardwood floors and French dormer windows. Breakfast is included.

Hôtel Le Germain

2050 rue Mansfield tel: 514 849 2050; www.germainmontreal.com; $$

Long one of Downtown's finest boutique hotels, Le Germain is awash in distinctive details, from local artwork to bamboo-and-cotton towels in the stylish bathrooms and goose-down duvets on the comfortable beds. It's pet-friendly, too.

Hotel William Gray

421 rue St-Vincent tel: 514 656 5600; www.hotelwilliamgray.com; $$

Classic meets contemporary at this charming hotel, housed in two 18th-century buildings overlooking the buzzy Place Jacques-Cartier. Two roof terraces deliver fantastic views, plus there's a spa, the Maggie Oaks brasserie and a cocktail lounge.

Niagara-on-the-Lake

Charles Inn

209 Queen Street; tel: 905 468 4588/866 556 8883; www.niagarasfinest.com/properties/charleshotel; $$$

This charming inn, dating from the 1830s, has all sorts of idiosyncratic features, from lovely verandas to old cast-iron fireplaces. There are 12 guest rooms, each decorated in a version of period style, and the beds are super-comfortable.

Lakewinds Country Manor B&B

328 Queen Street, at Dorchester; tel: 905 468 1888/866 338 1888; www.lakewinds.ca; $$

A well-kept garden with an outdoor heated pool is the jewel of this expansive 1880s Victorian mansion. Its six a/c

Moden styling in a Hilton Saint John suite

guest rooms and suites are each decorated in a particular style – Florentine or Singaporean, for example.

Toronto

The Broadview Hotel

106 Broadview Avenue; tel: 416 362 8439; www.thebroadviewhotel.ca; $$$

Old is new again at this impeccably restored boutique hotel in a landmark 1891 building. The Romanesque Revival-style architecture displays beautiful details inside and out, from terracotta carvings to vaulted ceilings to a glass-box rooftop.

Fairmont Royal York

100 Front Street West; tel: 416 368 2511, tel: 800 257 7544; www.fairmont.com; $$

When it was completed in 1927, the Royal York was the biggest hotel in the British Empire. It retains much of its original grandeur, especially in the sprawling lobby, which is decked out with mosaic floors and massive chandeliers.

Gladstone Hotel

1214 Queen Street West at Gladstone; tel: 416 531 4635; www.gladstonehotel.com; $$

A hipster hotel lies behind this handsome building dating from the 1880s. All 37 rooms have been designed by local artists, down to the wallpaper. Located in the most fashionable part of town, people come here to razzle it up.

The Ivy at Verity

111D Queen Street East; tel: 416 368 6006; www.theivyatverity.ca; $$$$

Toronto's classiest hotel is also one of the most distinctive: it's part of an old brick-walled chocolate factory and comes complete with an excellent restaurant. There are only four guest rooms, but each is decorated immaculately, with its own balcony.

Manitoba: Thompson

Best Western Thompson Hotel

205 Mystery Lake Road; tel: 204 778 8887; www.bestwestern.com; $

There's not much to choose between the main hotels in Thompson, making this standard higher-end motel as good a choice as any. Access to a steam room and small gym, and a cooked breakfast are included.

Manitoba: Churchill

Lazy Bear Lodge

313 Kelsey Boulevard; tel: 204 675 2969/ 866 687 2327; www.lazybearlodge.com; $$

Being log-built by hand (using lumber reclaimed from a boreal forest-fire), gives this hotel more character than other places in town. The restaurant is decent too (see page 114). Stays include a shuttle service from the station or airport.

Seaport Hotel

215 Kelsey Boulevard; tel: 204 675 8807; www.seaporthotel.ca; $

Fairly standard motel-quality the rooms may be, but overall this is the town's best-serviced hotel, with a dining room, coffee shop, sports bar and cocktail lounge on-site, and it's open year-round.

The Fairmont Royal York exterior

Saskatchewan

Ghostown Blues

Hwy 271, 2km (1.2 miles) west of
Maple Creek; tel: 306 661 8481;
www.ghostownblues.com; $
These lovingly refurbished cabins and
wagons, near Maple Creek, pose a wonderful opportunity to sleep on the range in
a piece of Prairie history. Choose between
the likes of cowboy cabins, 1870s sheep
wagons and a converted 1940s grain
truck.

The Resort at Cypress Hills

30km (18.6 miles) S of Maple Creek on Hwy
21 in Cypress Hills Interprovincial Park; www.
resortatcypresshills.ca/accommodations; $$
Choose between hotel rooms with
bathtubs and mini fridges, spacious
townhouses with lake views, or rustic cabins with their own fire pits – perfect for star-gazing. All accommodation
is within the park's grounds, for easy
access to the leisure facilities.

Alberta: Icefields Parkway

Deer Lodge

Lake Louise Drive, 3.5km (2 miles) west of
Lake Louise Village; tel: 403 522 3991; $$$
This 1920s log teahouse contrasts with
the pomp of its neighbour, Château Lake
Louise, a short walk away. Deer Lodge is
far more relaxed and focused on getting
away from it all. The rooftop hot tub has
fantastic views, and there's a sauna.

Simpson's Num-Ti-Jah Lodge

Mile 22, Hwy-93 N near Bow Lake; tel: 403
522 2167; www.num-ti-jah.com; $$$$
With its dazzling red roofs and Bow Lake
views, this is one of the most famous old
lodges in the Rockies. It was built in 1920
by legendary guide and outfitter Jimmy
Simpson (who lived here until 1972).

Vancouver

L'Hermitage Hotel

788 Richards Street; tel: 888 855 1050;
www.lhermitagevancouver; $$$$
The staff at this luxury hotel are famed for
their helpfulness and attention to detail;
other perks include a heated saltwater
pool, a stylish lounge, and free bicycle
use. Many of the suites come with fireplaces and stainless-steel kitchens.

SameSun Hostel

1018 Granville Street, at Nelson; tel: 604 682
8226/877 972 6378; www.samesun.com; $
SameSun has popular hostels in Kelowna,
Banff and the US: its zippy Vancouver
branch has 250 beds in four-, six- and
eight-bed dorms, and 11 private rooms.
It also provides a common area, lively bar
and a free continental breakfast.

Skwachàys Lodge

31 West Pender Street; tel: 604 687 3589;
www.skwachays.com; $$
You'll spot the totem pole that sprouts
from the rooftop before you arrive at
Vancouver's only First Nations-run
hotel, where each room is a unique art
installation created in partnership with
Indigenous artists and top Vancouver
hotel designers.

Inside the grand lobby at the Fairmont Royal York

Haida Gwaii

Haida House

2087 Beitush Road, Tlell; tel: 855 557 4600; $$$

Choose between a room in the Haida House lodge or an oceanfront cabin (for around double the price). Either way, this Haida-owned guesthouse on the bank of the Tlell River is ideally situated for nature-lovers: guided trekking can be pre-arranged.

Sword Fern Inn

3127 2nd Avenue; tel: 250 626 9299; www.swordferninn.com; $$

An intimate inn (previously Dorothy and Mike's), where the deck provides expansive views of the harbour from its hill vantage point. There's a fire pit and barbecue out in the lovely garden, and the place strives to be eco-friendly.

Dawson City

Aurora Inn

5th Avenue and Harper; tel: 867 993 6860; www.aurorainn.ca; $$

A sunshine-yellow exterior, cheerful staff and 18 immaculate en-suite rooms make this one of the best picks in town, plus it has a spacious restaurant and veranda (see page 117). Airport transfers are included.

Klondike Highway

Coal Mine Campground & Canteen

Box 110, 1 Mile North of Carmacks; tel: 867 863-6363; www.coalminecampground. com; $

A well-regarded campground on a bend of the Yukon River (it is possible to canoe here from Whitehorse), it has tent pitches as well as five cabins, complete with electricity and bedding. Coin-operated showers and firepits with wood are available.

Historical Guest House B&B

505 Wood Street, Whitehorse; tel: 867 668 3907; www.yukongold.com; $

This two-storey log home two blocks east of Main Street was built in 1907 for Sam McGee, the protagonist of a Robert Service poem, and his family. Two double rooms and a suite are available.

Yellowknife

Bayside B&B

3505 MacDonald Drive; www.baysidenorth. com; $

On the shore of Great Slave Lake, this quiet place offers a cabin and four rooms with an all-day café (Dancing Moose, see page 100) overlooking the waterfront, with a wraparound deck that provides a spectacular view of the bay.

Nunavut: Iqaluit

The Discovery

1056 Mivvik Street; tel: 867 979 4433; www.thediscovery.com; $$$

Boutique hotel The Discovery has a range of room types, from smart standard to executive suites – but all come with luxury bath amenities and high thread-count linen. Its centrally located downtown and offers a courtesy airport shuttle, too.

New Glasgow Lobster Suppers' main event

RESTAURANTS

The standard of Canadian cuisine has improved dramatically in the last few years. In the big cities there's a plethora of international and speciality restaurants; on either seaboard the availability of fresh fish and shellfish enlivens many menus, and even out in the country there's a liberal supply of first-rate, family-run cafés and restaurants.

If you're in a large city or town, choosing where to eat dinner is really just a matter of whatever takes your fancy – and is within your budget. You can find pretty much any type of cuisine in Canada's larger cities, with Montréal, Toronto and Vancouver especially standing out for their choice of international restaurants. Most run a dinner service starting at 5–7pm and ending at around 10–11pm. Expect to pay anywhere from $15–45 for a main dish at most places, and considerably more at fancier establishments. Almost everywhere you eat or drink, the service is fast and friendly – thanks to the institution of tipping (unless the service is dreadful, you should top up your bill by 15 percent or more).

Price guide for a two-course meal for one with a glass of house wine:
$$$$ = above $70
$$$ = $50–70
$$ = $30–50
$ = below $30

The list below is not intended to be comprehensive, but instead features our top choices, especially for evening dining, across the country.

Newfoundland
Big Stop
62 Trans-Canada Hwy; tel: 709 635 2130; $$
For meals in Deer Lake, close to the airport, this spacious dining attached to the Irving petrol station will keep you fuelled up. It serves a full menu of classic dishes (turkey dinners, grilled salmon), the obligatory fish and chips and hefty lemon meringue pies.

Java Jack's
88 Main Street North, Rocky Harbour; tel: 709 458 2710; www.javajacks.ca; $$
In Gros Morne National Park is this fabulous café, serving breakfasts such as lobster benny, well-priced lunches (try the salt cod fish cakes) and dinners such as salmon with peach and veggie lasagne.

Nova Scotia
Lobster Kettle
41 Commercial Street; Louisbourg; tel: 902 733 2723; www.lobsterkettle.com; $$$
Louisbourg's only waterfront restaurant is a solid bet for the local speciality, plus snow crab and signature seafood chowder. The pretty, red-roofed shack has an outside terrace where you can take in a view of the bay.

Sim's Corner oysters

New Brunswick

The Gables

143 Water Street, St Andrews; tel: 506 529 3440; $$

Located in St Andrews, this stylish little restaurant housed in a gabled, clapboard home built in 1870, serves fresh lobster, Bay of Fundy scallops, chowders and tasty burgers from its bayshore location. Seating overlooks the water.

Tops Pizza Restaurant

215 Union Street, at Sydney St, Saint John; tel: 506 634 0505; $

This old-school diner and Saint John favourite knocks out decent pizzas but also great lasagne, coleslaw and homemade soups – providing a filling lunch, often for less than $10. It's a booths and bar stools sort of place, and payment is cash-only.

Prince Edward Island

New Glasgow Lobster Suppers

604 Rte-258, New Glasgow; tel: 902 964 2870, www.peilobstersuppers.com; $$$

These famed lobster suppers have been running since 1958, with the usual gut-busting line-up of home-made rolls, seafood chowder, mussels and salad before the main event and ending with the "mile-high" lemon meringue pie (it's a set-price menu; pay at the door).

Sim's Corner Steakhouse & Oyster Bar

86 Queen Street, Charlottetown; tel: 902 894 7467; www.simscorner.ca; $$$

A stylish venue with exposed brick walls, on the menu at Charlottetown's town's top restaurant are delectable local oysters ($3 each), prime Canadian aged steaks (try the secret pepper sauce), and a huge choice of wines. The outdoor terrace hosts barbecues in summer.

Montréal

La Banquise

994 rue Rachel Est, Plateau Mont-Royal: www.labanquise.com; $

This shrine to poutine – Québec's earthy, folksy culinary symbol – opened in 1968 as an ice cream shop. Poutine first graced the menu in the early 1980s and the rest is history: there are now 30 poutine varieties on the menu.

Garde Manger

408 rue St-Francois-Xavier; tel: 514 678 5044; www.crownsalts.com/gardemanger; $$

A familial atmosphere fills this restaurant helmed by celebrity chef Chuck Hughes. Seafood is the speciality – the star being lobster poutine. A bustling bar and a cocktail-fuelled crowd make for one of the more vibrant dining spots in Vieux-Montréal. .

Tiradito

1076 rue de Bleury; tel: 514 866 6776; www.tiraditomtl.com; $$

This great restaurant brings heat, flavour and culinary sass to Montréal. The exciting small-plates menu is rooted in Nikkei – Japanese-Pervuvian cuisine. Seats encircle a large kitchen in the centre of

Cozy Lazy Bear Lodge

the dining room, which gives it a communal and intimate feel.

Toqué!

900 place Jean-Paul-Riopelle; tel: 514 499 2084; www.restaurant-toque.com; $$$$

Renowned chef Normand Laprise holds court here and the dining experience is ultra chic and unforgettable – if you can get a seat. Call far ahead to book – it's worth it; this is the restaurant that pushed Montréal to the top of the culinary ranks. Innovative dishes include a starter of a venison carpaccio with goats cheese followed by a main dish of suckling pig with squash gnocchi.

Wilensky's Light Lunch

34 avenue Fairmount oust; tel: 514 271 0247; www.wilenskys.com; $

Wilensky's is used for countless movie locations because the decor hasn't changed since 1932 – and that includes the till, grill and drinks machine. Sink your teeth into hot dogs with Swiss cheese or a chopped-egg sandwich and top off the meal with an ice-cream soda.

Niagara-on-the-Lake

Olde Angel Inn

224 Regent Street; tel: 905 468 3411; www.angel-inn.com; $$

With its low-beamed ceilings and flagstone floors, this is the town's most atmospheric pub. On the British-themed menu is filling and very affordable bar food, such as Guinness steak-and-onion pie and bangers-and-mash.

Treadwell

114 Queen Street; tel: 905 934 9797; www.treadwellcuisine.com; $$$

Focusing on the best of Niagara's produce, the farm-to-fork cuisine at this renowned restaurant includes pork belly with smoked apple and halibut with Ontario heirloom risotto. The local wines are equally excellent, as you'd expect from vineyard-country.

Churchill

Lazy Bear Lodge

313 Kelsey Boulevard; tel: 204 675 2969/ 866 687 2327; www.lazybearlodge.com; $$$

Attached to the log-built hotel (see page 109), Lazy Bear's restaurant focuses on "local," down to the windows recycled from an 1800s Hudson's Bay Trading Post. Meals include braised peppered elk and Manitoba bison. No alcohol is served.

Yellowknife

Taste of Saigon

4913 50th Avenue; tel: 867 873 9777l; www.atasteofsaigon.ca; $

Authentic Vietnamese dishes at this spacious, family-run restaurant, include stir-fries, rice vermicelli bowls and hearty pho, guaranteed to warm you up on a chilly day. It also offers a children's menu and takeaway for pick-up.

Trader's Grill

4825 49th Avenue in the Explorer Hotel; tel: 867 873 3531; $$$

Inside the brutalist building of the Explorer Hotel, the fine-dining experience

A generous salmon serving at the Lazy Bear Lodge

offers a refined menu with wide choice of northern food, including musk ox, caribou and lemon butter arctic char. It was voted the best Sunday brunch in town.

Zehabesha
5004 51st Avenue; tel: 867 873 6400; $
Traditional Ethiopian food is the last thing you'd expect in Canada's Northwest Territories, but the flavours at Zehabesha are striking and authentic. Meals include a vegan option, *misir wot* (red lentil stew). Fantastic value is an added bonus.

Toronto
Aloette
163 Spadina Avenue; tel: 416 260 3444; www.aloetterestaurant.com; $$$
Aloette's menu – and ambiance – is, in their words, "the neighbourhood bistro reimagined." Try roast squid with pork belly and Granny Smith apples, beef carpaccio with truffles and one of the finest burgers in town, crowned with Beaufort cheese.

Beast
96 Tecumseth Street, off King Street; tel: 647 340 8224; www.thebeastrestaurant.com; $$
What many outsiders have heard about the Toronto food scene consists of five letters: Beast. The meat-heavy operation is renowned for its whole animal dinners (advance notice is required), in which six courses are spun from every corner of the creature.

El Catrin
18 Tank House Lane; tel: 416 203 2121; www.delcatrin.ca; $$$
Not only is it coolly curated with a mural, punched metal lights and a wall of Day of the Dead skulls, but this eatery in the Distillery District has won awards for its mix of traditional and contemporary Mexican cuisine.

Lai Wah Heen
Metropolitan Hotel, 108 Chestnut Street; tel: 416 977 9899; www.laiwahheen.com; $$$
The high-end dining-room atmosphere at this Chinese restaurant is matched by a complex menu, best described as Hong Kong modern, with such dishes as fish with soy sauce, ginger and scallions. It's also noted for its dim sum (lunch only).

Rodney's Oyster House
469 King Street West, at Spadina; tel: 416 363 8105; www.rodneysoysterhouse.com; $$$
Toronto's favourite oyster bar, ensconced in a handsomely modernized old basement, serves up tonnes of the slippery delicacies, plus scallops, mussels, crab and shrimp. There's a good range of fresh fish too, always including salmon and trout.

Saskatchewan: Maple Creek
Rockin' Horse
103 Maple Street; tel: 306-662-2430; $$
Open for food Tuesday to Friday evenings, the big and hearty menu features mains like baby back ribs and chicken cordon bleu (served with vegetables or fries). Orange-painted walls, festoon lights and local art for sale enhance the warm atmosphere.

Joe Fortes seafood platter

Round Up

49 Pacific Avenue; tel: 306-662-3020; $
Popular with the locals, this friendly diner serves delicious homemade comfort food. The breakfasts are well-regarded, such as vegetarian omelettes and eggs benny. Riblets in honey garlic, BBQ or teriyaki sauce is also a failsafe choice.

Icefields Parkway: Lake Louise

Château Lake Louise

Lake Louise Drive, 4km (2.5 miles) west of Lake Louise Village; tel: 403 522 351; $$$
This grand hotel has several bars and restaurants, including the family-friendly Poppy Brasserie and fancy Alpine-themed dining room Walliser Stube, which specializes in fondue and raclettes. Dark wood-styling and views over Lake Louise complete the ambience.

Post Hotel Dining Room

200 Pipestone Road; tel: 403 522 3989/800 661 1586, www.posthotel.com; $$$$
Low ceilings and crackling fire create a cozy setting for a gourmet meal at this high-end hotel. The Swiss chef is big on rich meat and fish served with phenomenal sauces. The hotel's Outpost Pub is a less expensive option.

Vancouver

Bao Bei Chinese

Brasserie Keefer Street, at Main; tel: 604 688 0876, www.bao-bei.ca; $$.
Wildly popular for a reason, this upscale Chinese fusion spot packs in hungry diners every night. Standout items include handmade dumplings and the "kick ass house fried rice." It's a gorgeous space, with dim lighting and vintage design details.

Café Medina

780 Richards Street, Downtown; tel: 604 879 3114; www.medinacafe.com; $
Mediterranean-inspired cuisine and fresh-baked waffles make this café highly popular. Highlights include the salmon fumé (a ciabatta sandwich with eggs and avocado) and lavender lattes.

Joe Fortes Seafood and Chop House

777 Thurlow Street, near Robson; tel: 604 669 1940; www.joefortes.ca; $$$
This long-established oyster bar/chophouse/seafood restaurant is a city institution, with a summer patio upstairs, lively atmosphere and irrepressible maître d', Frenchy. The restaurant plays the food straight and in generous portions. There are daily lunchtime deals, too.

Vij's

3106 Cambie Street, 3km (2 miles) south of Downtown; tel: 604 872 3707; www.vijs.ca; $$$
One of Canada's best-known restaurants, its menu has a host of favourites, including lamb popsicles, Indian street food snacks, and locally distilled spirits at the bar (where you might find yourself waiting, as reservations are not taken).

Wildebeest

120 West Hastings Street; tel: 604 687

Joe Fortes' bistro–style interior

6880; http://wildebeest.ca; $$$
Possibly the quintessential Gastown restaurant, offering nose-to-tail dining, excellent brunch and moreish craft cocktails. Although it's an unashamedly meat-centric restaurant, vegetarians are also well-taken care of. If you have the marrow, ask for a "sherry luge" chaser.

Haida Gwaii

Queen B's

3208 Wharf Street, Queen Charlotte; tel: 250 559 4463; $
The welcoming Queen B's is a beloved local hangout, offering fine breakfasts, lunches and savoury snacks, and dinner on Friday evenings. Outside, you'll find tables with water views; inside is a cozy, eclectic vibe with lots of local art.

Dawson City

Aurora Inn Restaurant

5th Avenue and Harper Street; tel: 867 993 6860; www.aurorainn.ca; $$
This relaxed hotel restaurant serves wood-fired meats, burgers, seafood, schnitzel and a handful of tasty vegetarian mains, such as pasta and salads. For breakfast, there's a European-style breakfast buffet. It's even better in summer, thanks to the raised deck area.

Klondike Kate's

3rd Avenue and King Street; tel: 867 993 6527; www.klondikekates.ca; $$
The excellent Klondike Kate's is the friendliest, most relaxed place in town for fabulous breakfasts and dinners (its

salmon specials are not to be missed). The restaurant is such an institution that it even sells branded merchandise.

Whitehorse

Antoinette's

4121 4th Avenue; tel: 867 668 3505; www.antoinettesrestaurant.com; $$
Chef Antoinette moved from Trinidad and Tobago as a teenager and has become renowned for her comfort food with a Caribbean twist. Highlights include Crispy Guacamole Salmon and Curry Chook Stew. Tapas are available 2–6.30pm.

G&P on Main

209 Main Street; tel: 867 668 4708; www.gandpsteakhouse.com; $$$
This family-run dining room, 40-years-old but replanted on Main Street from the Alaska Highway, is among the most friendly local fine-dining establishments. Steak and (deep-dish) pizza are the stars, but there's also pasta, salads and seafood.

Nunavut

Frob Kitchen & Eatery

Frobisher Inn Astro Hill Complex, Iqaluit; tel: 867-979-222; www.frobisherinn.com; $$$
The Frob Kitchen & Eatery lays claim to the best Sunday brunch in the North. Open from dawn til dusk, Chef Felix Le Cavalier serves gourmet dishes including maple syrup-glazed arctic char, tenderloin steak and a couple of Thai vegetarian options. The Inn also has a casual pub-eatery, the Storehouse Bar & Grill.

NIGHTLIFE

It's no surprise that Canada's nightlife is centred around its three major cities. Montréal hosts a range of festivals, from jazz to theatre, and performing arts are as widely available as you'd expect in a city so culturally dynamic.

Toronto is known for its live music across all genres – many a band has forged their career performing on the city's stages. In September, the 480,000 people who descend for the film festival give the city an extra buzz.

Vancouver has a famously vibrant nightlife, from raging nightclubs to sophisticated bars and craft beer taprooms (South Main – the stretch of Main Street between East 2nd and East 33rd avenues – is a hub for craft brewery tasting rooms).

Elsewhere, there's folk music, theatre venues and late-night bars to keep you entertained into the night. The clubs, bars and venues listed are all accessible from places in the itineraries.

Nova Scotia

Louisbourg Playhouse
11 Aberdeen Street; tel: 902 733 2996; www.louisbourgplayhouse.ca
If you're wondering what an Elizabethan theatre is doing in Louisbourg, it was built by Disney in 1994 as a set for its film *Squanto: A Warrior's Tale* and donated to the neighbourhood. Inspired by the Globe Theatre in London (on the inside, at least), there's an intimate atmosphere to

enjoy the music, comedy, plays or dance, on nightly during the summer. Shows start at 8pm (box office from 2pm).

Les Foufounes Électriques
87 rue Ste-Catherine est; tel: 514 844 5539; wwwfoufounes.qc.ca; daily 3pm–3am; $
Known as Foufs, this is the best place in Québec for alternative bands, attracting a crowd from ravers to punks. Its huge outside terrace perfect for summer evenings, and pitchers of beer are cheap.

Prince Edward Island

Confederation Centre of the Arts
145 Richmond Street; www.confederation centre.com.
Charlottetown's centre for performing arts hosts an extensive variety of acts, from rock and jazz through to comedians, magicians, theatre, opera and ballet. The centre is also the home of the main show of the annual Charlottetown Festival (mid-June to Sept), which is a musical adaptation of *Anne of Green Gables* (mid-June to August) running since 1965 (other than a break due to Covid-19 restrictions).

Olde Dublin Pub
131 Sydney Street; tel: 902 892 6992; www.oldedublinpub.com
A beloved Charlottetown institution, this is a justifiably popular spot serves a range of imported and domestic ales – Guin-

ness and Kilkenny included. The signature Irish Cocktails are good value (try The Lucky Leprechaun: coconut rum, melon and pineapple juice). Catch the live folk music – mostly Irish – from Fridays to Sundays, during May to September.

Montréal

Club Soda

1225 boulevard St-Laurent; tel: 514 286 1010, www.clubsoda.ca; open nightly for shows, generally from 8pm until closing, though times vary; $$

Large live-music venue Club Soda attracts all the best acts and has reached almost legendary status in Montréal. It also hosts Jazz Festival and Just for Laughs shows and burlesque.

Le Mal Nécessaire

1106B boulevard St-Laurent; tel: 514 439 91991; www.lemalnecessaire

A subterranean tiki bar incongruously located in Chinatown (look for the glowing green pineapple), this laidback hipster joint channels old-school Hawaii, serving fruity drinks to a funky hip-hop and house soundtrack, often by a live DJ. There's also outdoor seating for those summer evenings.

Place des Arts

Quartier des Spectacles; entrances on 1600 rue Saint-Urbain & 175 rue Sainte-Catherine West; tel: 514 842 2112/1 866 842 2112; www.placedesarts.com

The jewel of the Quartier des Spectacles, Place des Arts *is the* biggest cultural and artistic complex in Canada. It delivers a comprehensive year-round programme of dance, music and theatre: regular concerts are staged by the Orchestre Symphonique de Montréal (www.osm.ca), Orchestre Métropolitain (www.orchestre metropolitain.com) and L'Opéra de Montréal (www.operademontreal.com).

Pullman

3424 avenue du Parc; tel: 514 288 7779; www.pullman-mtl.com

Much like the premium wine it pours, this bar hits all the right notes: warm, elegant, casual. The innovative interior includes a wine-glass chandelier, rich woods and industrial-chic exposed concrete walls. Among the vast wine repertoire, you'll find some Québécois vintages; it can be challenging to find local wines at the bars, so this is a good place to try them.

Théâtre Rialto

5723 avenue du Parc; tel: 514 770 7773; www.theatrerialto.ca

This grand old theatre with a glorious Beaux Arts facade dates back to 1923–24, and is designated a National Historic Site of Canada. It hosts varied programming throughout the year, from theatre to opera to concerts.

Toronto

Bar Chef

472 Queen Street West, at Augusta; tel: 416 868 4800; www.barcheftoronto.com

More than 5,000 housemade bitters grace the walls of this cool, candlelit bar.

This spot attracts cocktail connoisseurs – the concoctions aren't cheap at $16 and up, but they're served and prepared every which way and always with innovative flair. Also impressive is the variety of European absinthe. Dress up – it's the place to see and be seen.

Cameron House

408 Queen Street West, at Cameron tel: 416 703 0811; www.thecameron.com
This legendary venue, located just west of Spadina Ave, is unmissable – you can't fail to notice the colourful murals on the outside. The interior is a clash of Beaux-Arts boudoir and honky-tonk bar, and the stage at the back of the room has long provided a showcase for emerging talent of every genre.

Horseshoe Tavern

370 Queen Street West, at Spadina; tel: 16 598 4226; www.horseshoetavern.com
Many Toronto bands got their start here, and it's still a favourite for the newly famous to play a set or one-off concert. The interior of the Horseshoe Tavern (on the scene since 1947) is relentlessly unglamorous, but the low cover charge is a major compensation.

The Rex Jazz & Blues Bar

194 Queen Street West, at St Patrick; tel: 416 598 2475; www.therex.ca
In arguments about which is the best jazz club in town, this one (with an attached restaurant and hotel as well) is consistently near the top of the list. A well-

primped crowd lounges in the spiffed-up interior, but any reservations about pretensions evaporate once the (always top-notch) music begins. There are usually two shows a night, at 6.30pm and 9.30pm.

Vancouver

Alibi Room

157 Alexander Street, Gastown; tel: 604 623 3383; www.alibi.ca
Alibi is a hip bar-restaurant, filled with beer-loving locals and those who have travelled to pay homage to one of Vancouver's best spots for beer, thanks to its menu of at least 50 ever-changing craft varieties on tap. Weekend brunch is a popular option.

Fortune Sound Club

147 East Pender Street, Chinatown; tel: 604 569 1758; www.fortunesoundclub.com
If you're looking to hit the dancefloor, this is the place: all types of Vancouverites mingle at this Chinatown dance club spinning old-school hip-hop, soul, house and others till the wee hours. It has the best sound system in the city. Expect a $15 cover charge on weekends, and get there before 11pm to avoid a long line.

MIA

350 Water Street, Gastown; tel: 604 408 4321; www.areyoumia.com
Conveniently located in happening Gastown, MIA attracts some of the city's top DJs and live performances across two dramatically-styled rooms. The dress code is decidedly stylish.

Head to a club night in Vancouver

Queen Elizabeth Theatre

630 Hamilton Street, at Dunsmuir Street; tel: 604 665 3050; www.vancouver.ca/theatres. The main focus for the city's performing arts, this Downtown venue hosts visiting theatre, opera and dance troupes as well as the occasional rock concert. It's one of four venues run by Vancouver Civic Theatres, along with the Orpheum, Vancouver Playhouse, and the Annex.

Dawson City

Bombay Peggy's

2nd Avenue & Princess Street; tel: 867 993 6969; www.bombaypeggys.com.
Hotel bars provide more sedate alternatives to the gambling hall, and the lounge at Bombay Peggy's hotel stands out for its fine atmosphere and style. The Naughty Martinis menu brings a host of drinks with eyebrow-raising connotations – but the bartenders here know their stuff, so ask them for a recommendation. Summer brings live music from northern and national artists.

Sourdough Saloon

At the Downtown Hotel, 2nd Avenue and Queen Street; tel: 867 993 5346; https://downtownhotel.ca/sourdough-saloon The Sourdough Saloon is popular with locals and visitors alike, partly thanks to its gimmick of the Sourtoe Cocktail, which includes the ingredient of a real pickled human toe. If it touches your lips, you receive a certificate. Live piano performances enhance the frontier-town atmosphere, from 7–9 pm in summer.

Whitehorse

Frantic Follies at the Westmark Whitehorse Hotel

4051 4 Avenue; www.franticfollies.com
The widely touted Frantic Follies vaudeville act stage shows of banjo-plucking and frilly-knickered-dancing at the Westmark Whitehorse Hotel have been playing in town for around three decades. It's a fun, two-hour romp through the era, with parts of the show built around the works of the Bard of the Yukon, Robert Service (late May–early Sept Tue–Sun 8.30pm).

Yellowknife

Top Knight

4910 49 Street (Upstairs); tel: 867-920-4041 Located above the Scottish-themed Black Knight Pub, this little-known venue kicks into action from 5pm with sports on TV (and a family night on Saturdays), before becoming a nightclub and live music space. The pub downstairs offers a huge collection of Scotch (somewhere around 120).

Nunavut

NuBrew

2025 Iqaluit Lane, Iqaluit; tel: 867-979-2337; http://nubrewbeer.ca
NuBrew is the taproom of Canada's northernmost microbrewery, Nunavut Brewing Company. As well as a place to try the northern lagers and IPAs available from keg, can and bottle, this sociable venue hosts live bands, board games and trivia nights.

Science Fiction & Fantasy

BOOKS AND FILM

From the early days of Mary Pickford and Lorne Greene, to Pamela Anderson, Jim Carrey, Jason Priestley, the Ryans (Gosling and Reynolds), and Elliot Page, Canadian actors, producers, and writers have found success in Hollywood. Larger-than-life heroes Superman, Ghostbusters, and Rambo originated from Canadian-born authors. Ottawa-born comedian Dan Aykroyd even made a tongue-in-cheek feature film about the Canadian plot to take over the Hollywood empire, while Ontario-born Mike Myers launched Austin Powers at the world. Such figures are recognized internationally. Canada's French-language films consistently win international accolades, and Toronto and Vancouver vie for the title of Hollywood North, with a ready supply of skilled professionals and the great locations that can replicate big American cities.

The list of important Canadian writers alive today is too long to enumerate, but a few worth exploring include first Canadian Nobel Prize in Literature winner Alice Munro (2013), Margaret Atwood, Joseph Boyden, Douglas Coupland, Rohinton Mistry, Yann Martel, Bev Sellars, and Michael Ondaatje. The diversity of the country supports their staying "home" and allowing their writing to reflect their place in the world. Writers' festivals provide Canadian authors with the opportunity to crisscross the country to promote their books and meet their readers. Canadian festivals attract international writers as well, whose publishers recognize that Canadians are avid readers and a good market for their stable of authors.

Film

Made by Canadians
Mon Oncle Antoine (1971). My Uncle Antoine follows 15-year-old Benoît for a coming of age story in a mining town in the Asbestos Region of Québec. One of Canada's most highly regarded films.

C.R.A.Z.Y. (2005). Multi award-winning Québécois masterpiece about a young French-Canadian growing up amid strong homophobia during the '60s–'70s.

Bon Cop, Bad Cop (2006). Dark comedy-thriller: two cops – one from Ontario and the other from Quebec – resolve to overcome their individual prejudices to solve a murder case.

Incendies (2010). Oscar-nominated for Best Foreign Language Film, mystery-drama Incendies is a tale of twins retracing their late mother's past in the war-torn Middle East.

Anne of Green Gables (1985). Internationally beloved made-for-television drama film based on the 1908 novel of the same name, set in PEI.

Filmed in Canada
One Week (2008). Ben Tyler (Joshua Jackson) embarks on a cross-Canada

Canada has a rich literary heritage

motorcycle journey after being diagnosed with cancer.

Scott Pilgrim vs. the World (2010). Shot entirely in Toronto, slacker bass guitarist Scott (Michael Cera) wins the girl by defeating her seven exes.

Brokeback Mountain (2005). This American epic is set Wyoming, but the scenery of ragged mountains, lakes and evergreens belong to the Canadian Rockies and southern Alberta.

Books

Fiction

The Handmaid's Tale by Margaret Atwood. The society of hyper-patriarchy imagined by Canada's most eminent novelist continues to be relevant long after its 1985 release (and wildly popular TV series).

The Chrysalids by John Wyndham. A science-fiction classic built around a group of telepathic children and their adventures in post-Holocaust Labrador. First published in 1955.

Generation X: Tales for an Accelerated Culture by Douglas Coupland. This celebrated Canadian novelist defined a generation via the stories of three drifting 20-somethings, including this seminal 1991 title.

No Great Mischief by Alistair MacLeod. This evocative novel tells the tale of a family of Gaelic-speaking Nova Scotians from Cape Breton. Undoubtedly one of the best Canadian novels of the 1990s.

Lives of Girls and Women by Alice Munro. One of the world's finest living story writers, Munro deals primarily with the lives of women in the semirural and Protestant backcountry of southwest Ontario – including in this '70s novel.

A Complicated Kindness by Miriam Toews. Novels set in the Amish/Mennonite communities were very much in vogue in the mid-2000s – and this version, set in Manitoba, is one of the best of its type. The protagonist is a 16-year-old girl rebelling against the strictures of her community.

Travelogues

Smalltown Canada by Stuart McLean. A well-known author and radio host takes his readers on a cross-country tour of small-town life in seven communities across Canada, presenting a humorous, rich portrait of the people.

Beauty Tips from Moose Jaw by Will Ferguson. A funny account of the writer's three-year journey around Canada using every mode of transportation – from helicopter to canoe – imaginable.

City of Glass: Douglas Coupland's Vancouver by Douglas Coupland. The cult author turns his pen to his hometown.

Passage to Juneau: A Sea and Its Meaning by Jonathan Raban. Raban documents his 1,000-or-so-mile journey from Seattle up the Inside Passage to Alaska.

Sacré Blues: An Unsentimental Journey Through Québec by Taras Grescoe. A spicy, irreverent examination of a unique part of North America, with nary a mention of a politician. It explores the heart of contemporary Québec and how it relates to its neighbours.

ABOUT THIS BOOK

This *Explore Guide* has been produced by the editors of Insight Guides, whose books have set the standard for visual travel guides since 1970. With top-quality photography and authoritative recommendations, these guidebooks bring you the very best routes and itineraries in the world's most exciting destinations.

BEST ROUTES

The routes in the book provide something to suit all budgets, tastes and trip lengths. As well as covering the country's many classic attractions, the itineraries track lesser-known sights. The routes embrace a range of interests, so whether you are an art fan, a gourmet, a history buff or have kids to entertain, you will find an option to suit.

We recommend reading the whole of a route before setting out. This should help you to familiarise yourself with it and enable you to plan where to stop for refreshments – options are shown in the 'Food and Drink' box at the end of each tour.

For our pick of the tours by theme, consult Recommended Routes for… (see pages 6–7).

INTRODUCTION

The routes are set in context by this introductory section, giving an overview of the destination to set the scene, plus background information on food and drink, shopping and outdoor activities.

DIRECTORY

Also supporting the routes is a Directory chapter, with our pick of where to stay while you are there and select restaurant listings; these eateries complement the more low-key cafés and restaurants that feature within the routes and are intended to offer a wider choice for evening dining. Also included here are some nightlife listings and our recommendations for books and films about the destination.

ABOUT THE AUTHORS

This book was compiled by freelance travel writer Siobhan Warwicker. Based near Northumberland, England, she is at home with dramatic weather and big landscapes – and Canada has captured her imagination lifelong. An American Studies graduate, she regularly travels across the pond and was editor of the latest Rough Guide to Canada.

CONTACT THE EDITORS

We hope you find this Explore Guide useful, interesting and a pleasure to read. If you have any questions or feedback on the text, pictures or maps, please do let us know. If you have noticed any errors or outdated facts, or have suggestions for places to include on the routes, we would be delighted to hear from you. Please drop us an email at hello@insightguides.com. Thanks!

CREDITS

Explore Canada

Editor: Sarah Clark

Author: Siobhan Warwicker

Head of DTP and Pre-Press: Rebeka Davies

Head of Publishing: Sarah Clark

Picture Editor: Piotr Kala

Cartography: Katie Bennett

Photo credits: DestinationCanada 8MC, 16; Fogo Island Inn 26ML, 68, 104ML, 106, 106/107; Hilton Hotels & Resorts 104MC, 108/109; Joe Fortes 4MR, 116, 116/117; Lazy Bear Lodge 114; Shutterstock 1, 4ML, 4MC, 4MR, 4MC, 4ML, 4/5T, 6TL, 6MC, 6ML, 6BC, 6/7T, 7MR, 6/7M, 7MR, 8ML, 8ML, 8MC, 8MR, 8MR, 8/9T, 10/11, 12, 12/13, 14, 15L, 14/15, 16/17, 18, 19L, 18/19, 20, 20/21, 22, 23L, 22/23, 24/25, 26ML, 26MC, 26MR, 26MC, 26MR, 26/27T, 28/29, 30, 31L, 30/31, 32, 32/33, 34/35, 36, 37L, 36/37, 38, 38/39, 40/41, 42, 42/43, 44, 45L, 44/45, 46, 46/47, 48, 49L, 48/49, 50/51, 52, 52/53, 54, 55L, 54/55, 56/57, 58, 58/59, 60, 61L, 60/61, 62, 62/63, 64, 65L, 64/65, 66, 66/67, 68/69, 70, 71L, 70/71, 72, 72/73, 74, 75L, 74/75, 76/77, 78, 79L, 78/79, 80, 80/81, 82/83, 84, 85L, 84/85, 86, 86/87, 88, 89L, 88/89, 90, 90/91, 92, 93L, 92/93, 94, 94/95, 96/97, 98, 99L, 98/99, 100, 100/101, 102, 103L, 102/103, 104MR, 104MR, 104MC, 104ML, 104/105T, 108, 110, 110/111, 112, 112/113, 114/115, 118/119, 120/121, 122/123

Cover credits: Capilano Suspension Bridge *Shutterstock*

Printed in China

All Rights Reserved

© 2021 Apa Digital AG

License edition © Apa Publications Ltd UK

First Edition 2021

No part of this book may be reproduced, stored in a retrieval system or transmitted in any form or means electronic, mechanical, photocopying, recording or otherwise, without prior written permission from Apa Publications.

Every effort has been made to provide accurate information in this publication, but changes are inevitable. The publisher cannot be responsible for any resulting loss, inconvenience or injury.

DISTRIBUTION

UK, Ireland and Europe
Apa Publications (UK) Ltd
sales@insightguides.com

United States and Canada
Ingram Publisher Services
ips@ingramcontent.com

Australia and New Zealand
Booktopia
retailer@booktopia.com.au

Worldwide
Apa Publications (UK) Ltd
sales@insightguides.com

SPECIAL SALES, CONTENT LICENSING AND COPUBLISHING

Insight Guides can be purchased in bulk quantities at discounted prices. We can create special editions, personalised jackets and corporate imprints tailored to your needs.
sales@insightguides.com
www.insightguides.biz

INDEX

MAP LEGEND

- ● Start of tour
- → Tour & route direction
- ···· Extra tour
- ❶ Recommended sight
- ❷ Recommended restaurant/café
- ★ Place of interest
- ❶ Tourist information
- ✈ Airport / Airfield
- ❋ Ferris wheel
- ✚ Hospital
- ⊙ Metro - Montréal
- Ⓜ Metro - Toronto
- Ⓢ Skytrain - Vancouver
- 🚌 Bus station
- Ⓜ Museum
- ✚ Church
- 📖 Library
- 🎭 Theatre
- ⚊ Statue
- 🅿 Parking
- Lighthouse
- ⚑ Beach
- ▲ Summit
- ❋ Viewpoint
- ⊖ Border crossing
- ––– Ferry route
- ━·━ International border
- ––– Province border
- Park
- Important building
- Urban area
- Transport hub
- Glacier
- National park